The Portable Storage Handbook

The Complete Guide to Starting, Owning, and Operating a Portable Storage Business

Anders Norlin and Phil Herndon

Edited by Glenn McMahan, Endeavor Literary Services, LLC
Cover and interior design by Rebecca Finkel, F+ P Graphic Design

ISBN softcover 978-0-692-07489-3

Contents

Preface

PHIL HERNDON

I AM WRITING THIS on the day that a grieving group of friends and family will be gathering to mourn the loss of our friend and colleague Anders Norlin. I worked with Anders for more than twenty years, and during that entire time my friend was fighting cancer. Anders's first cancer diagnosis was in 1995. Thanks to his unshakeable desire to live and to improve methods of cancer treatment, Anders survived those years well.

This book is dedicated to Anders and to people like him for whom a safe, healthy, and secure life is a goal rather than a reality. Striving for that goal becomes their form of peace. Anders did not complain. He was positive. In his Swedish style, Anders regularly quipped, "That is that and on we go." He once said that upon learning that he would need a new round of treatment that would challenge his peace for the coming months.

I am truly humbled by the determination that Anders continually displayed. I wonder if I have the character to face such a difficult path the way he did. Anders did not let disease rule his life; instead, he endeavored to live the best life he could while holding the disease at bay. I am better for knowing such a man.

Anders and I started writing articles for the National Portable Storage Association in 2003. This book is an edited collection of those articles. There was a day last November when I visited Anders in the hospital. It was clear he was in his final round. While holding his head in pain and nearly deaf, he looked at me and said, "We knew this day would come." He had finally surrendered and conceded to his enemy. In a feeble attempt to cheer him up, I reminded him that we still needed to publish our collection of articles. I told him I had an article I needed him to review. All I got was a brief, weak smile. That last conversation has been my motivation to undertake this project. Anders and I hope that it serves our industry well.

Introduction

Maybe you are one of those people who woke up one day, bought five containers, painted them, put your name on the sides, and decided to go into the portable storage rental business. If so, you know that getting started is tough. When we started our business, we had a lot of questions and there was no place to find answers. We had to tough it out, spy on our competitors, or spin our wheels until we figured it out.

The Portable Storage Handbook is meant to serve as a resource for finding the answers to questions that new or experienced operators might have, and as a teaching tool for you and your staff.

Here are some basic questions operators should ask when starting a portable storage business:

Where do I buy containers? You can buy them from leasing companies, shipping lines, traders, one-way shippers, private parties, and even your competitors. Chapter 3 is a good place to start building your plan on rental equipment.

What are the options for moving containers? Trucks and trailers is the short answer, but we'll deal with those options more in chapter 3.

How do I determine rental rates, billing cycles, and depreciation? While the fundamental business is simple, finance issues can create big challenges. At best we are avoiding taxes (legally) and at worst we are spending more than we are taking in. Look to chapter 7 for help!

How do I get the phone to ring? Sometimes you can "fake it until you make it," but not in this case. Without customers you do not have a business! Chapter 4 deals with marketing.

What kind of a yard should I have? You should consider two factors: The amount of space you need and your purpose for that space. Some operators have a full-blown operation with modification, sales, and inventory. Others have a simple place just to store rental equipment. Chapter 2 has some useful information on this topic.

What can I do if someone does not pay me? This is not an uncommon problem and time is not on your side! Read up on collection tricks in chapter 7!

How do I get financing for business growth? Your options include friends, family, private lenders, banks, and vendors. Look to chapter 7.

How large of an area should I serve? Some operators find plenty of business within a fifty-mile radius and others need 150 miles. It's important to consider all the factors discussed in chapter 2.

Is an industry association helpful for my business? The simple answer is yes, but if you need more convincing read chapter 12!

This book is a combination of experience and shared knowledge from other companies in the industry. It's also written to address a changing business environment. It's important to understand the fluid nature of this business. Some things remain constant while others may fluctuate dramatically. This is part of what makes owning and operating your business fun. However, remember that change can make or break you. So please don't consider this book as gospel.

There are plenty of resources for how to start a business, but we will focus on the nuances of starting and operating a portable storage business. Soon you will find satisfaction when you turn the corner on your first year and you can drive around town and see your containers earning money.

If you find that your experience in the portable storage business is different than what is presented in this book, please look to the NPSA for methods of providing feedback and sharing useful information with like-minded operators. At the time of this writing, the NPSA is utilizing Google Groups to share appropriate information about new and different operating ideas.

Finally, if this book puts you to sleep, be thankful; it may be a more economical approach than other ways to fall asleep! However, if you find the portable storage business interesting, and if you enjoy learning and growing, then we welcome you into our group and look forward to hearing your story in the years to come.

CHAPTER 1

Operations

OPERATING A PORTABLE STORAGE BUSINESS can be simple. You can just sit at a desk and pay a contractor to store, repair, and move your equipment. However, in the early days of my operation, I was anxious to grow. So, I asked an experienced friend if he knew the secret to growing the business. He said I should control everything. This chapter and the next two chapters assume that you directly control each element of your business.

Setting Up a Shop

PHIL HERNDON

How much stuff do you need? We recently took inventory and discovered that we had about twice the shop equipment and tools we

needed. Here are some thoughts on how much equipment you need for a growing rental fleet and to sustain moderate-to-complicated modifications.

The Shop

We have a canopy that measures 30-feet wide and 48-feet long that rests on two containers. Wind and rain still get in, but it is a lot cheaper than building a building! To move boxes into our shop, we use a heavy-duty pallet jack at one end and a shop lift at the other end. The single most critical element is probably a flat shop floor. If the floor is not level, you will constantly struggle to align doors and make simple modifications. As an alternative, a delivery truck or trailer can be used to move equipment in and out of a shop.

The Big Tools

We have four welding machines and one plasma cutter. Some of these machines are better for heavy work and some are better for fast work. If the welders only had one, they would choose the 180-amp, 220-volt single-phase MIG machine (wire feed, flux core). Plasma cutters are cool machines, but many shops will use an angle grinder fitted with a cut-off blade, just because it is easier to set up. For an air compressor, we run a 3-horsepower electric unit with an 80-gallon tank. If demand is high, we are fortunate to have a 5-horsepower gas-powered unit. For painting, our work-horse is a gas-powered airless that can run two guns no problem. For cleaning, we have a gas-powered high-pressure washer and an electric, diesel-fired steam cleaner. We also have three 6-kilowatt gas generators that allow us to work in our yard away from the shop.

The Little Tools

We destroy angle grinders regularly. After looking at other options, we agreed that buying four $80 grinders per year was okay. Each mechanic gets his own grinder with his name and the date he got it written on the tool. Sawzalls, chop saws, port-a-powers, acetylene torches, and big hammers are always needed.

Minimal Equipment?

If all you plan to do is install lock boxes, wind turbines, and an occasional rollup door, a good welding machine (180 amp or larger) with a durable paint rig could be all you need. We tried the airless sprayers from Home Depot and they did not hold up. I know several rental operators who have a service crew come on site to complete modifications and prep rental boxes. That may be an excellent solution for many operators.

Regardless of what equipment you have or need, remember that every container sale or rental that leaves your yard reflects you and your company. Why not let it make you look good?

Setting Up a Yard

We have two yards. One is about one hundred miles north of our main yard. Both yards are fenced and graveled. One, a simple acre in size, is a yard without staff. It just has a lock on the gate. We keep one container forklift at that site. Our main yard (two acres) is where our office, trucks, and shop are located. The key elements for a yard include site security, flat gravel or paved surfaces, enough room for a tractor-trailer to drive through or turn around in, and a sign.

Shop Forklift

We have a 5,000-pound pallet-sized propane shop lift. It's fine for most shop projects and has solid tires. Requirements for a shop lift include at least six inches of ground clearance so it does not get stuck in the yard, a side shift, and a horn so mechanics know you are there even above the shop noise. Ours is used for moving containers in and out of the shop, unloading supplies, lifting one end of a container, pulling reefer cooling units, and occasionally letting visiting kids drive it for fun!

Container Forklift

If you can only have one, get a forklift that will safely lift a container and use it in the shop when it's needed! You'll want one that has 7-foot forks (minimum) with an 8-foot spread to safely move a box. Because most lift capacity is measured two feet off the mast and the load from a container that is 8-feet wide is centered four feet off the mast, you are best to double the capacity of lift.

So, a lift rated at 15,000 pounds is good for lifting a 7,500-pound 40-foot container. Oddly, many lifts can raise a load to a height of just two inches below the top of two stacked standard containers. In other words, you won't be able to stack containers three high. If you need to do that, a two-stage mast will do the job. Also, it's not advisable to stack three high with a lift unless the containers have fork pockets. We find that an older, simple lift suits our service just fine.

You will be wise to have a backup plan for how to operate without a forklift for a day or two because even with good maintenance your lift will go down. It will take a day or two to get it back up. Availability of parts and service are an important consideration for choosing a lift. Back when I worked at the shipping line terminal, we blew a transmission and had to wait two weeks for a transmission that was air freighted from Sweden!

Our thirty-year-old Hyster serves us well. It has 8-foot forks, a 20,000-pound capacity Detroit diesel, and minimal electrical things to go bad. Since most operators have gravel or dirt yards, it is critical to regularly change the oil and filters. We replace a hydraulic hose about once a quarter. We have a local hydraulic repair shop that matches what we bring in much faster than trying to source OEM. Also repacking or rebuilding hydraulic cylinders on our lifts and delivery trailers seems be needed once every six months.

Container Side Pick

A side pick is necessary if your storage yard is stacked three high or if you have more than one hundred containers in storage. Our lift can stack containers four high although we normally only stack three high. Because I dislike paying an employee to watch another employee work, our drivers load and unload their trucks. We are migrating to solid tires for all our lifts to avoid flat tires. If you don't use solid tires, use deep, thick-tread, off-road industrial tires.

Painting Containers

Your rental fleet should look the best it can, and exterior paint is an important element in providing a quality image. Direct-to-metal, water-based industrial coatings provide the easiest application and a reasonable coating life. We have rental boxes that were painted fifteen-years ago and still look good.

Our direct-to-metal paint comes from and industrial paint supplier. The product is water-based, acrylic enamel with a coverage of 225-square-feet per gallon. We buy 55-gallon drums of stock gray, beige, and white paint. This is a one-coat system. To prepare the surface, we use a steel wire cup brush to remove surface rust. We scrape off any aging decals or flaking paint. Water-based coating cannot be applied when the humidity is above 75 percent, and in California that only happens when it's raining. High humidity will cause the paint to dry with a rust bloom because the water in the coating cannot be released into the air as it dries. If that happens, you will just have to recoat the box.

Once the surface is cleaned and prepped, we apply a thin fog coat across the entire box. We usually let the box sit for at least an hour. Then we inspect it for any last-minute surface problems and apply a full coat over the box. We paint the roofs and open the doors to coat the jams all the way around. We have found that a mat finish works best because it obscures dents on a used box and reduces glare.

On a good day with reasonable conditions, our painter can prep used boxes and coat two 40-foot or four 20-foot containers in the shop. A good painter can make the work look easy and a not-so-good painter can leave you with a mess.

Container Modifications

I have a weakness for modifications. Putting 20-foot and 40-foot containers out on-rent is not very exciting for me. If my business only allowed me to do that, I'm not sure I'd be in it! However, from the business side, rental makes a lot more sense than modifications. Rental is reoccurring and standardized whereas modifications are customer-specific and seldom reoccurring. Because modifications can cause financial loss, it's important to take a careful look at how this work will impact your profitability and business.

Are modifications helping you achieve your business objectives? We remind ourselves every day that we are here to rent portable storage. Although we sell and modify boxes, we still have container rental as our main objective. We don't let modifications take preference over rental. If we need to make 15-foot rental boxes, we will pull these modification projects from the shop to make room for rental needs. Don't shoot yourself in the business foot by letting modifications distract you from your rental business.

There is a broader business benefit to modifications. They allow us to have the shop, tools, staffing, and skills that enable us to quickly react to rental opportunities. If we only offered rentals, we would need substantially fewer employees, trucks, and inventory. We could do that, but after looking at the numbers, I don't believe that approach would help us. We would lose operating bandwidth and not be able to serve our rental customers like we do today.

Our modifications customers are rarely also our rental customers, so modifications increase our market footprint, allowing more people and companies to know who we are and giving us access to opportunities that could develop into rental business. We just delivered six heavily modified containers to a concert/event center. While there I noticed several rental containers. I made sure that the site manager would call us for future rental needs.

Know Your Modification P&L

I regularly dissect my income statement, breaking up revenue and costs into sub-classes for sales, modification, rental, and trucking. I know that we could add class codes to QuickBooks and get the software to do the work, but doing it myself helps me see the numbers. Modifications are not a cash cow, but they help us keep the lights on!

We also analyze each project, looking at hours worked and material costs. This helps me see where my quote may have been overly optimistic. I don't expect every project to be a home run. Sometimes it's more about seeing the finished project. Last month we completed a 20-foot build-out that included rollup doors, a ladder, flooring, track lighting, and large speaker boxes at each end. Then we delivered the box to a company that mounted it to a low trailer. The box went to a company that is outfitting the interior to look like a store. It will be a mobile showroom for a consumer electronics company. Fun? Yes. Profitable? I doubt it.

Years ago, I worked for a guy who marked up everything by 20 percent. He ignored the market and any discussion about perceived value. Sometimes he underbid the rest of the world and other times he was so overpriced that there was no response from the solicitor. As you develop experience and learn how to do a wide variety of modifications, your pricing will become realistic and you will be profitable.

Getting the Basics Right

My car mechanic is only open Monday through Thursday. He does not change any fluids and will refer more work to others than anybody I know. He knows what he does best, focuses on that, and sends the rest of the work elsewhere. I really like the guy and can always count on him to take care of our vehicles or send us to someone who can!

It's no different at our company. Early on we tried to seize every opportunity. We soon realized that we were spending all our time in "school," always learning new things but never reaching a proficient level or becoming profitable. Fortunately, as we dabbled in new opportunities, we also began to learn where we were capable and where we weren't.

Looking back, we can clearly see how our skill set has developed. What was difficult three-years ago, is now much easier. Sometimes the work requires no supervision. For example, we set up 20-foot containers at a job site office for a customer with very detailed requirements. The customer wanted tiled floors, full electrical, insulation, air conditioner/heater, paneling, and trim. It all came together to make a very nice office. We met the customer's needs.

However, we installed, removed, and reinstalled 50 percent of the interior paneling. We spent days trying to find the correct floor tile. What was supposed to be a simple electrical installation was not simple at all. We kept tracking dirt into our work. We learned a lot, but it was an expensive lesson. The most important lesson was to do our best to avoid modifying to a customer's exact specifications, and instead to offer standardized components. Here are some examples:

Electrical

We offer a simple electrical package with two 4-foot fluorescent lights and one duplex outlet next to the light switch. This includes a simple 12-gauge plug that connects to an extension cord outside the container. This arrangement meets 90 percent of our customer's electrical needs and we can do the work efficiently. When a customer asks for more than that, we include a sub-panel and begin to provide separate circuits for the additional items, such as an air conditioner or additional electrical outlets. All this can be done within conduit and wall-mounted junction boxes.

Doors

We offer a 36-inch steel slab door and we build the jam/frame. Again, that approach accommodates almost all our customers and we only need to worry about sourcing one door size. We have found that our local building supply store keeps the doors in stock, so we only buy the doors as needed. For the deadbolt and door latch, we use medium-priced keyed-alike sets; again off-the-shelf.

Windows

Simple 3-foot by 3-foot double-pane vinyl windows seem to be our mainstay. We fabricate a steel frame, stitch-weld that into a hole in the container wall, and then screw and caulk the window in. This approach is simple, provides plenty of light, and can easily be replaced if the glass is broken. Our security bars are half-inch steel square stock welded to the outer steel frame.

Wind Turbine

Due to the corrugation of dry container roofs it was taking a tube of caulk to seal the turbine flange to the container roof, so we began installing a square frame in the roof and mounting the turbine to that.

Side Vent

Some customers want more ventilation than a wind turbine, so we offer side vents. Our local building supply store stocks simple 12-inch by 12-inch louvered/screened vents that work well and are still small enough to preserve security. The installation process is similar to the process for windows.

Plan Table

We offer a plan table that is constructed from shop-grade or better plywood with a fabricated steel frame support that is mounted to the interior front wall. This is simple, functional, and adequate for most job site offices.

Rollup Doors

We stock 6-foot rollup doors. I have a friend who only stocks 7-foot doors, but we each do our best to direct the customer to the door we have in stock. Our rollup door supplier will supply any size door with a lead time of only a week and a half. However, doing our best to keep orders at 6-foot doors simplifies the process for our shop and maximizes our profitability through efficiency.

The End Result

Because of our standardization practices, modification quoting is done on a component basis. Any of us in the office can provide a quick and simple quote without delay. This keeps our shop busy and profitable, keeps materials and parts inventory to a minimum, and reduces waste.

In developing your strategy to standardize modifications, remember that the NPSA has a host of associate members who supply components for almost any container modification you can imagine. Before the association existed, many of us were dealing with vendors who did not offer products tailored to our industry. Also, the Google Group single-site email forum, available through the NPSA, is a great way to learn about new ideas and methods from fellow operators.

Condensation in a Container

The dew point is the temperature at which moisture in the air turns to liquid, causing the accumulation of dew on surfaces. When we see dew in the morning on our lawn it is because the cool night temperature has caused moisture in the air to change from vapor to liquid. This can be a regular occurrence inside containers. Dew can cause water damage or mildew if steps are not taken to prevent it. The problem is more common in humid climates, but all operators should be aware of the condition and know about the solutions.

The inside of a storage container is a micro-climate with its own weather system. When a storage container is closed-up, the amount of moisture inside the container remains relatively constant with very little air exchange. This closed environment means a leak or any condition that introduces moisture into the container will raise the humidity inside the micro-environment. Additionally, the single-layer steel walls increase the ability for large temperature swings within a container. Finally, the wood floor can act like a saturated sponge that prolongs the presence of moisture in the container and allows the moisture to increase the humidity inside the container.

Let's look at the some of the causes and cures for this pesky problem.

Case 1: The Contents

Way back when I was shipping containers, my company had a major customer that imported canned goods. Unfortunately, between loading in Asia and unloading in the US, the steel cans filled with pineapple developed surface rust. An investigation determined that the wood pallets carrying the cans were made of wet, green wood. As the pallets dried, the moisture was expelled into the container and had nowhere to go. The humidity inside the container increased causing the dew point to fall. Eventually, vapor condensed on the steel cans. By including moisture-absorbing material inside each shipment, we eliminated the problem.

Introducing moisture-laden contents into a closed storage unit can be a big problem. The high school grounds crew who park the riding mowers in your container every night with fresh-cut grass caked on the mowers' undersides is a recipe for a wet seat the next morning! The best solution is increased ventilation. Roof whirly vents work well. In extreme cases, low side or end vents are needed to get the job done.

Case 2: How it is Packed

We built a nice steel shed to hold a friend's dirt bikes with an upper shelf for his large gear bags. The bags fit so snuggly on the shelf that there was no air circulation behind the bags. At night the steel container wall cooled rapidly creating condensation in the dead air space behind the bags. Eventually, there was a mold problem.

When a storage unit is packed tightly with no room for air to circulate, and when interior surfaces cool below the dew point, there will be moisture and mold problems. The simple solution is to repack the container. If the contents can't be repacked to facilitate better air circulation, then you might consider ways to protect or insulate the affected area so that the dew point is not reached.

In a recent conversation with an NPSA member who had this type of problem, I learned that he struggled to improve air circulation. We agreed that one option was to use some type of ducting to provide increased circulation. Another option is to use humidity reducing products that are available from several industry suppliers.

Case 3: The Outside

We sold two containers to a customer. One had a regular problem with condensation inside the container and the other did not. Both containers were watertight and held the same mix of contents. It was determined that one container had a full western exposure that allowed the afternoon sun to heat the box. Because air expands as it is heated, moist air was expelled from the container during the day. Additionally, the contents and the container walls retained some of that heat. The overall affect was that the western-facing container was on average warmer and much drier than the shaded container next to it.

In a similar case several years ago, a windproof and watertight container was placed at the base of a slope, on a level school playground. No one could find a leak, but the container was continually experiencing moisture and mold problems. After several visits, we found that the area under the container was collecting the water that was draining off the hillside. The moisture was making its way through the floor and into the container.

Moisture buildup caused by exterior conditions can be rectified by removing the exterior cause (moisture under the container), reorienting the boxes (so that they get stronger sun exposure), or introducing a desiccant as in case 2 above.

Case 4: Container Condition

I recently visited a job site where one of our office containers was leaking. Water was getting through the window frame. We found that the caulk had split on the upper edge of the window connected to the steel frame joint. Many caulks will shrink as they cure. Container movement can cause a caulked seam to separate. So, we removed the old caulk and applied a new bead well within the seam.

Although we all like to think our rental and sale equipment is the best available, it is not perfect. Sometimes we walk the roofs. Even the smallest water leak will cause major dew problems inside a container. A moisture-soaked floor will also create problems. Old containers with plank floors allow for more air circulation and fewer condensation problems. Additionally, fluctuations in ventilation will have a significant impact. Many of the containers we purchase arrive with the side vents taped closed. Although there is not a large amount of air exchange through these splash-proof vents, they do have benefits, especially over time in a closed container.

Serving Our Customers

In the end it comes down to service. We can't afford to let our customers deal with moisture problems on their own or they will begin to seek new providers. Learn the basics first, understand the causes, and then partner with your customer to solve the problem. Remember that the value in temporary portable storage is not the storage equipment, but what is being stored!!

Shipper-Owned Container (SOC)

A shipper-owned container (SOC) is used by the person or entity who owns the cargo inside the container and who also owns the container. This is different than a regular shipment in which the shipping line owns (or leases) the container.

To make a sale container an SOC, if the box is unmodified, the process is simple. These containers are often used by, for example, a person moving to Hawaii or a relief group that is serving needs in West Africa. The first-time operator needs to know the challenges of this process. After reading this section, you can hopefully be a resource for the steps in this task. When this type of customer calls us, we review the following steps with them and confirm that they really need a shipping container at their destination. Here are the basic steps:

1. Determine that an SOC can be carried by the shipping line going to the desired destination.
2. Choose a container size.
3. Have the container neutralized and surveyed for being cargo worthy (info below). Give the inspection certificate to the customer who will forward it to the shipping line.
4. Arrange for the empty container to be loaded onto an intermodal chassis and delivered to the customer's cargo loading point. If the customer wants to load the box first and then lift or crane it onto and intermodal chassis, that's fine; just don't let crane standby charges be your problem. Place a cargo seal on the container, which is available from the freight forwarder.
5. Hire an intermodal drayage company to move the container on a chassis to the pier or railyard for shipment overseas.

Once the container arrives at the port of discharge, the customer or the agent will need to arrange delivery and off-loading of the container from an intermodal chassis. This process can be very costly because shipping lines rarely offer a tariff discount for SOC shipments. Most of the time, the need for a container at the final destination is not justified due to the cost of this method. Also, be sure to confirm the duties charged for bringing your own container into a foreign country. The rates can be 30 percent of the container cost.

Be realistic. It may not make sense for you to offer this type of equipment. The customer hand holding, equipment issues, knowledge of SOC requirements, communication with freight forwarders and rail and marine terminals can collectively be a consuming task.

For customers requiring a modified container for shipment overseas, the process becomes even more complicated. We enjoy this business because it's a nice diversion from installing lock boxes on rental containers. We have modified containers for battery storage, research labs, submarine transport, water treatment plants, and sometimes even a mystery shipment! If you take on this type of work, there are some factors to consider so that the container can still be shipped as a container. First the basics:

- **Don't violate the structural frame.** If the container cannot be picked up, stacked, or locked together with other containers, it cannot be shipped the same way all the other 200,000 million containers moving around the world are shipped. It can still be shipped, but only as special cargo. Handling fees, the risk of damage, and security for the cargo become major issues.
- **There can be nothing extending outside the eight corners of the container.** If there is, it impacts the ability of the stevedores to stack the container on a ship above or below deck. Containers with protrusions can be shipped, but it will require special handling. The freight rate will include charges for the surrounding stacking spaces that cannot be used.
- **No openings.** The modified container must be watertight and secure. We will often put a temporary steel plate over an opening or window when the container is being shipped. Screwed and sealed in place, this works for most requirements.
- **Securable hatches** can be used also.

Container Solutions

- **Unit Number.** This is the four-letter prefix followed by six digits and a seventh digit known as the check digit. The four-letter prefix is an indication of the equipment owner (e.g. MAEU=Maersk) and most shipper-owned containers use XXXU or NONU. The unit number is the owner's choice. The check digit is calculated by an algorithm based on the prefix and six-digit unit number. BIC, or BIC-CODE.ORG is the company that registers and protects container prefixes. Its website has a check digit calculator and other useful information about container identification. The unit number must be displayed on 4-inch high decals or stencil, visible from all four sides and the roof.

- **Data/CSC Plate.** This plate mounted on either door. It provides manufacturer data, ownership, certification, and inspection status. Once you modify a container, it is decertified. In years past, many shipping lines would not sell containers unless the Data/CSC plate was removed. Today, for modified shipper-owned containers, the original plate remains unless the box goes through a new certification process. Each CSC plate has a location for proof of inspection.

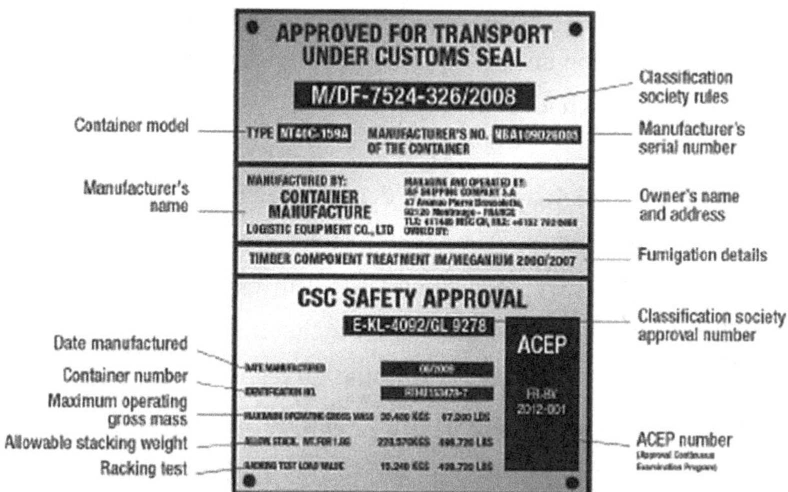

Image Source: https://www.bic-code.org/csc-plate

- **Weights.** On either door, the container tare and max gross weights need to be identified in kilograms as well as pounds. Because shipping lines typically calculate cargo weight from the loaded container weight less the tare weight, these numbers are important for getting your customers' containers onto a ship!

- **Crazy stuff.** When a customer requires modifications that seem to be over-the-top, such as removing a full side or nose panel, we first will say it can't be done. If they see no alternative, we bring in our surveyor (more information on the inspection below) as he/she will be the person who approves the container for ocean transport.

The Actual Cargo-Worthy Inspection

We work with a local qualified inspector who provides surveys for a fee. In addition to surveys of shipper-owned containers, the surveyor also reviews depot repair estimates on behalf of the shipping lines and leasing companies. He or she also completes condition surveys and fleet condition audits. To find a surveyor in your area, you should be able to call a local depot and ask them who they use for surveys.

The survey is a completed form that identifies the basic container information (size and type) and then certifies it as acceptable for ocean transport. The surveyor will update the inspection plate on the container with an ACEP sticker to show that the box has been inspected. You'll need to confirm with the surveyor how long the survey is good for, but they are typically valid for six months. The inspector will give you the original survey. We normally scan and send it to the customer. He or she forwards it on to their freight-forward company or directly to the shipping line. Most shipping lines require a cargo-worthy certificate before the container can be physically delivered to the terminal.

This part of our business is not large, but is good shop work, helps us develop skills, and allows us to do new things that conventional modifications do not require.

Cargo-Worthy Surveys

On the West Coast, there are surveyors in Seattle, Oakland, and Long Beach. All three are industry professionals with years of experience who provide an accurate inspection when I need containers in those locations. Around the world there are similar people who, for a fee, provide this valuable, independent service. They are:

- **Long Beach:** Stan Carew of CCMS
- **Oakland:** Edi Birsan of EDI, Inc.
- **Seattle:** John Fanning of CCI

I asked them some important questions and compiled their answers below. I hope that you find this information helpful. If you need clarification or take issue with the discussion below, contact me or one of the surveyors.

1) Who defines "cargo worthy"?

Although the Coast Guard has national authority, enforcement is difficult. To compound this, some shipping lines and leasing companies have their own definition of what is cargo worthy. In a *de facto* fashion, it is the surveyor who decides what is cargo worthy. While groups like the IICL have established standards for container condition, there is no clear industry established definition for cargo worthy that is enforced across the industry.

2) What are the basic elements of a CW survey?

Left largely to their own, the surveyor's approach is all about safety. The structural integrity of the container is the first question. Any damage, corrosion, or wear and tear could impact the container's ability to carry cargo. This requires a full view of the underside of the container as well as the sides and roof. Also, the surveyor must confirm that the container fits within the ISO dimensions. The surveyor confirms that the container is windproof and watertight, that the doors function properly, that the flooring is solid, and that the box is reasonably clean. Finally, the markings and identification are confirmed. If the container is found to be suitable, a new ACEP sticker is applied by the surveyor to the CSC plate on the door.

3) Who is qualified to be a surveyor?

There is no specific test to become a surveyor. The IICL has an inspector's certification test, but that does address cargo-worthy condition. Experience is key to surveying containers. Often there are conditions or combinations of damage that require an inspector's judgment learned only by years of experience and accumulated knowledge.

4) How long is a survey valid?

For equipment in an active managed fleet, the official CSC survey interval is two-and-a-half years. At the SOC level, surveys are valid for three-to-nine months, depending on location, the surveyor, and the shipping line. A safe rule would be three months, unless there is an agreement with the line transporting the container to extend that period.

5) How can I get a survey done in my region?

If there is no local surveyor, the requestor has no choice but to shoulder the transportation cost of bringing a surveyor to the equipment.

6) Can I get a loaded container surveyed?

Yes, but with caveats. Should the box require any welding or significant repair, there is a good chance the cargo will have to be unloaded.

7) Anything else?

It can be beneficial to tell the surveyor about the type of cargo being shipped, especially if odor inside the container is a potential issue. Plan ahead! Give the surveyor enough time to schedule an inspection with the depot and fit the work into his or her schedule. Finally, container surveyors are some of the nicest people in the world (let the reader judge for himself!).

Finish Strong

I could fill this book with stories about projects I would have preferred to not have done. As I write, we have three projects that have not gone as planned. In each case, we have had to agree to finish the project no matter what it takes. I usually fade first. I get tired of the changes and details, and then I have to watch my attitude with the customer. Sometimes the customer is the problem, in which case we have to sit down and agree on a fair way to finish the project. Recently, I had a very large payment being withheld because a rollup door had a dent in it. I was not even sure we caused the dent. In the end we pulled the door, took it to an auto body shop, had it repaired, and had the paint color matched!

Difficult jobs that make you feel like you are being tortured are the odd beginning of a long-term positive relationship with clients. I've had customers come back to me with more business even though we faced problems with the first project. We reviewed what went wrong the first time and maintained a productive relationship.

All in all, modifications have been good for our business and we further our common goal of raising the bar for our industry. More than fifteen-years ago, at an NPSA event, I explained what a lock box is and how it works. Things have changed since then. What we can do with a container today is cool and amazing. Let's keep building and sharing our experiences!

CHAPTER 2

Storage Rental

Contracts and Tracking

PHIL HERNDON

Container sales can provide a strong financial return, but portable storage rental offers many benefits that are hard to ignore. Any established operator would be remiss to not rent containers. The opportunity to purchase a container at a wholesale price, install a lock box, paint it, add your decals, and rent it to a customer is hard to pass up. However, if it were that simple, there might be as many portable storage rental companies as there are Starbucks stores! This chapter will shed light on the rental side of our business.

The Rent Contract

Few things between you and your customer can to be more beneficial than a contract signed by both parties that clearly establishes responsibility for the care and keeping of your equipment at the customer's location. Some might argue that a rental contract can easily be nullified in court. Others might argue that most customers just sign it and never read it. But a contract is still your most powerful tool for understanding and recourse in case of a dispute between you and the customer. You could have your attorney draw up an agreement, but we have printed below the model we use. For NPSA members, there is a sample contract on the association's website. As most companies in the portable storage industry have done, we asked friends for a copy of their contract and then edited it for our use. In our case, I believe that shorter (one page) is better. I detest fine print and legalese. Use a contract from day one of your interactions with customers, otherwise you could wake up one day and realize you have a lot of catching up to do!

Here are some of the benefits of using rental contracts:

1. It is a clear agreement between you and customer.
2. Should you need to take legal action against your customer, it is the starting document for your claim.
3. It can be tailored for each customer's situation. You might include a large security deposit or allow the customer to move the unit, if required.
4. Contracts are a great way to demonstrate your control over your assets.
5. Should you sell part or all of your fleet someday, contracts give a potential buyer the confidence of your control of the fleet you wish to sell.

We keep our contracts in both physical and electronic files. Once a customer signs the contract we normally just file it; seldom do we get asked for an executed copy.

Rental Fleet Tracking

Ten years ago, we rented ten 40-foot containers to a customer. That business had finished a conversion project, but they also fell in love with our containers, so they off-hired six units and kept four. For some reason we continued to bill them for six and did not catch the error for three years! Another customer who had twelve boxes on-rent, called to off-hire a box. That was fine, but when we looked in our system we realized that that box had been used for two years without us billing them! Accounting systems are great, and dispatch systems lifesavers, but without an inventory control system, you are wide open for these types of over-or-under billing! Additionally, these mistakes can be more significant as your business grows!

There are several NPSA associate members who provide inventory control systems. Some even include billing and dispatch functions. Attending an NPSA conference and visiting each of these vendors is a good starting point for choosing the system best for you. Connect with a few fellow members to get feedback on what system they use and how it works for them.

Other benefits of a fleet tracking system include:

- Real-time data on the composition of your rental fleet. Knowing the size, type, and location will help you understand you market penetration.
- Your depreciation calculations are much easier if you have a real-time database of your inventory.
- Calculating unsecured property tax for multiple tax jurisdictions is a breeze of you can run a report that divides your inventory by location.
- If you have storage yards, occasionally you need to build inventory in one yard or bring equipment back to the main yard to sell off. Being able to see the detail for a box needing off-hire helps in those kinds of decisions.

Your rental fleet is most likely the most valuable portion of your business. Many operators have retired quite comfortably by selling their rental fleet. If you don't control this part of your business, it will be very difficult to benefit from it! Recently I was asked to consider purchasing a failing competitor's rental fleet. When I physically surveyed the equipment on-lease I found that less than 60 percent of the inventory was where it was supposed to be. It was a mess. Don't be caught in this position; it will adversely impact your cashflow and the value of your inventory.

Inventory Control

ANDERS NORLIN

In today's world, technology is a big part of all businesses. But in the portable storage container business, inventory control technology can be trumped simply by looking out the window at the container yard. A high stack of containers means business is slow, and a low stack of containers means business is good.

However, there is more to it. Inventory control means knowing where all your sale and rental containers are, and ensuring they are all accounted for, at any given time. The containers in your rental fleet and in your sales inventory should to be accounted for, for several reasons.

Operationally, you need to know what is coming off-rent and when, what is going on-rent and when, and what is staying on-rent. Furthermore, you need to distinguish between containers that can be sold when off-hire and containers that cannot be sold when off-hire.

For accounting purposes, you need to know what is being billed, for what period, at what rates, as well as what changes in the billing is the result of on-hires and off-hires.

The financial prospective requires that you know how much you paid for your containers, when you purchased them, and how much all of them have depreciated in relation to Generally Accepted Accounting Principles (GAAP) and for tax purposes.

To maintain good inventory control, you need a good system. Several software programs are suitable for portable storage companies, ranging small to large, which can be found among NPSA's members. You can also create your own system by using a combination of basic software, such as QuickBooks, and Microsoft Access or Microsoft Excel.

Physical Inventory Reconciliation

It doesn't matter how good of a system you use, unless it is properly implemented, and that your company has a good discipline for using it. The reports produced by the system(s) should properly reconcile to the physical inventory. For instance, you need to check the yard inventory report against what is physically in the yard at a specific time. Some operators do this quarterly. At the same time, you should check the on-hired inventory against the list of containers that you are collecting rent from. You do that by looking at the rental agreements and check that there is a corresponding invoice for each container.

In addition, you need to do site inspections and confirm the whereabouts of your rental containers. If your rental fleet is relatively large, it is not feasible to travel around and check on all hired containers on a quarterly basis. However, it is good practice to communicate with or visit slow-paying customers frequently to make sure the container(s) they rent from you are at the location indicated in the rental agreement. One can assume that a paying customer has his or her container. That may not always be true, but it is more likely that a non-paying customer will not have his container. Occasionally, you may want to confirm the location and inspect containers that have been on-rent for a long period of time.

The total physical container inventory is the number of containers in the yard(s) plus the number of containers out for rent.

Financial Inventory Reconciliation

Your financials reflect the container fleet in two places. First, on the profit-and-loss statement as rental revenue, and second, on the balance sheet as fixed assets.

It is good practice to reconcile the amount of the monthly or twenty-eight-day billing to the physical container inventory, and to the rental agreements that generate the revenue. You should also reconcile the accounts receivables to the actual container(s) for which there is an outstanding invoice.

For the balance sheet reconciliation, you should have a list of containers at their cost or capitalized value, which corresponds to the total value of the fixed assets. Furthermore, you should have a list of containers showing the accumulated depreciation. The key is to do your accounting on a per-unit basis so that you can see, at any given time, what the cost of a container is, how much it has depreciated, and what the cost of goods sold would be if you sold the container.

Tax Inventory Reconciliation

This reconciliation is similar to the financial inventory reconciliation for the balance sheet. However, the accumulated depreciated value for each container should be the tax depreciation rather than GAAP depreciation. These numbers are not very important for day-to-day operations, but they are a necessity at tax times or when you want to sell your business.

If you run your balance sheet on a per-container basis, there should be a schedule to your tax return that shows the accumulated depreciation for your entire rental inventory, as well as each individual unit.

Mobile Self-Storage and White Boxes

PHIL HERNDON

I confess that I am not excited about mobile self-storage. The idea of taking possession of someone's belongings is the big rub for me. The beauty of portable storage is that I have no connection to what is inside my box that is on-rent. It is delivered empty and comes back to me empty. Writing these articles provides a healthy way to examine my thinking, and maybe I am wrong in resisting the opportunities that exist in this area. So, my goal here is to write with the intention of settling the jump-in or stay-out question. As I write, I don't know where this will end!

In my mind, there are three factors to consider: the physical, the financial, and the customer. Let's deal with each in that order.

Physical

Trucks: My trucks are all designed to move empty boxes and they are all tilt-bed. My 20-foot trucks have beds that are six inches short of carrying a 20-foot box with all four corners on the bed (a requirement for carrying a loaded container). So, we can do this if we limit this business to 10- and 15-foot containers. This assumes the customer is willing to live with the contents tilting slightly during pickup and delivery.

Dispatch/Trucking: We are at an operational level that allows our trucks to do more and more off-hire to on-hire moves. This type of move occurs when one customer's rental off-hire goes directly to another customer's on-hire. With MSS, we'll reduce those opportunities and get less work done per truck. That's because more truck-moves require more yard-stops than with simple portable storage.

Lifts: I have a 10-ton lift and a side pick. So we should be OK here, unless we are storing someone's law library.

Service Area: We serve a market that is two hundred miles from one end to the other, and we have two satellite yards where equipment is stored. We would only be able to use our main yard for loaded storage (assuming we change our use permit) since the other yards do not have onsite personnel. Additionally, the cost to move boxes from our farthest rental areas back to our main yard would be time consuming. It would be best to limit our service area for MSS.

Storage Yard: Our yard has a use permit that allows for storing only empty containers. To change that may take years and thousands of dollars in fees. I am also not sure what the fire department requires. I'll have to investigate what the extra cost would be.

Financial: Our rates are based on portable storage. Even if we double our rental, pick up, and delivery rates, I am not sure how profitable MSS will be. I do know that even if we double our empty rates we would still be well under the big MSS national competition. We regularly talk to customers who are in shock at the price difference between us and PODs.

Bottom-Line Impact: About six or seven years ago, I worked with one of the national MSS companies offering a franchise in our area. After two trips to meet with them and countless spread sheets, I could not make the numbers work. The obstacle was the cost of the branded storage units and the franchise fees. In this analysis, neither of those are factors, which is significant.

Capital Expense: If we only use 10- and 15-foot boxes that we already have in fleet and add more as needed, then the need for capital will not be that significant and the equipment acquired could be used empty or loaded.

Customer: Regarding homeowners, I recently completed an on-hire to a private party that took fifteen emails, one site visit, and multiple phone calls. Once the container was delivered, there were three emails about a neighbor's complaint. Then, when I was jogging through the neighborhood, another neighbor grabbed me and suggested that our truck drove onto her lawn. A simple psychological analysis would reveal that I am not wired for these types of transactions.

MSS will require our sales staff (other people than me) to become more patient and understanding. Our drivers will have to focus more on proper placement that minimizes impact to neighbors. Our shop will have to more thoroughly clean each box and make sure it is free of odors. All of this is doable stuff, but we'll have to adjust.

Legal: We would need a modified rental agreement. Not a big deal. My current general liability policy would need to be expanded to cover loaded containers. Just more money.

Conclusion

Sorry, I am not jumping into this, at least not now. But this does not mean I am closing the door. I choose as a long-term strategic direction to investigate each of the obstacles and work toward making MSS part of our future. I have several friends in the NPSA, whom I highly respect, who might accuse me of not being aggressive enough. It's true that ten or fifteen years ago, I would have gone for it hard and fast. But today I have plenty of responsibilities. I can wait, plan, and make the change to MSS in good time.

CHAPTER 3

Container Pick Up and Delivery

MOVING CONTAINERS is an integral part of the business. It is *portable* storage after all! The storage that we offer is at the customers' locations, and in almost all cases at ground level. So, specialized equipment is required to complete the function. Recently, a head-strong friend chose to enter a business heavily dependent on trucking. Without wise counsel, he underpaid his drivers, and ignored highway log books and overtime rules. He was in shock when drivers quit, and he was threatened with fines and the cancelation of his operating authority. These problems don't even mention the impact it all had on serving his customers. If you can't serve your customers, you will lose them.

Should You Own and Operate Your Own Trucks?

PHIL HERNDON

In 1999, when I had just started my company, I had the usual clean desk and silent telephone. Although I was committed to growing the business, I was also confident that I did not want to own or operate trucks! In two previous experiences, I had endured late-Friday phone calls from drivers with equipment problems, people claiming my truck hit their car or caused property damage. It seemed unrealistic to expect anything positive to come from operating my own trucks.

Today, thanks in part to the relationships developed through the NPSA, I have converted. Hearing from fellow members who have expressed the benefits of owning the transportation part of a rental business has changed my approach. That transition was not easy, and I learned a few lessons along the way.

Lesson 1: If you must use an outside trucking service, do your best to have a regular driver and truck, and that you dispatch that truck yourself. Dealing with a dispatcher who works with multiple drivers who are driving different trucks will add up to a pile of frustration for you and your customer.

Lesson 2: Use excellent equipment. I have used delivery trailers that dropped the container off the back a full two feet to the ground. I had a roll-off bed that would slide on its own (while going down the freeway). We have seen delivery trailers that looked like they had been farm implements in another life!

Lesson 3: Hire quality drivers. I had a door nearly torn off a truck and the driver could not explain what happened. I had a contract driver abandon a trailer three hundred miles away from the destination because he was having a bad day. I have watched a band of difficult drivers bounce from company to company.

Lesson 4: Build in flexibility. One of the best ways to grow a rental fleet is to be able to deliver a container quickly. Letting the customer decide when they need a rental box delivered is critical. Years ago, when I asked a friend to reveal the key to building a rental fleet. He was quick to say, "Own or fully control your delivery."

So here I am today: I own and operate trucks. They are as new as I can afford, and they are in pretty good condition. I get positive feedback about my drivers and we stay busy. Now, when my driver is one hundred miles away with a blown tire, I don't get rattled. While I am still not a fan of trucking, I see it as necessary for the business.

What Does Trucking Cost?

I am sure all of us cringe when we pay the fuel bill for our trucks. We spend a lot of money on fuel and that will not change. But it never hurts to look at the total cost of operation and know roughly what an hour of trucking costs you. When I add up truck loan payments, insurance, fuel, maintenance, wages, and worker's comp, a typical month of operation cost us $9,500 or about $50 per hour, or roughly 95 cents a mile, with an average speed of forty-five miles per hour. Then, looking at the revenue side, I have calculated that we bill just over $11,000 per month per truck. I would encourage each operator to go through the same exercise.

One of the big benefits of being part of the NPSA is the ability to compare notes! I shared my trucking cost numbers with four other NPSA members. Here is their feedback:

- *East Coast Member:* He has higher costs because he runs all new equipment with the ability to carry heavy loads. He is also in a very congested traffic area.
- *Midwest Member 1:* He owns the trailers and hires power (no, not "higher power"!). This frees him to focus on rental. It has worked well because he has had the same trucks and drivers for more than three years. His is fine with this as a break-even part of his business.

- *Midwest Member 2:* They operate like I do and see similar numbers. They have good drivers and see the benefit of operating their own trucks.
- *Gulf Member:* His operating numbers are higher, and revenue is lower because he is in a more rural area with fewer "backhaul" opportunities.

We can conclude from this little survey that there is no one formula for trucking success. It depends on several factors: local market, rental equipment mix, internal resources, and complementing opportunities. We all learn as we go.

As your fleet grows, you will need to regularly evaluate your trucking needs, costs, and revenue. In our accounting system, we make sure that our trucking costs and revenues are accurately coded so that we can see the cost of trucking.

What Truck Should I Buy?

When purchasing any vehicle, the upfront questions are: What am I going to use it for and what can I afford? Other issues include increases in business, driver overtime, and the need to respond to customer delivery requests. Finally, being on-site at your business helps you know the equipment mix and the needs. Simple logic says that you can usually deliver the smallest storage unit with the largest truck, but the reverse is not possible. Typically, your first truck should be a tractor trailer, capable of delivering a 40-foot container (or the largest storage units you have).

Choices between new trucks, used trucks, or leasing are best made with the help of your accountant, banker, and equipment supplier. Over the years, we find that financing new trucks through a bank or dealer suits us best. When I make that last payment, it's nice to know that the truck is mine. Buying a new truck spares us from issues related to the previous owner's actions.

One thing that drives me nuts about trucks is dealer mechanical service. Maybe it only happens in California, but there is no way you can have a truck serviced at the dealer in less than three days! Because of this, choosing the most reliable make and model is critical. Once you grow to be a multiple-truck operation, make sure you have an extra truck. That will relieve the pain of protracted visits to the dealer for service.

Our 20-foot delivery truck is basically a standard flatbed tow truck. Requirements for this truck include automatic transmission, air suspension, and a 22-foot steel deck bed. We modify the bed for container securing and we have rails to guide the box off the bed. Hino's model 258 is a very common flatbed tow truck that works for containers. However, we learned that the Hino model 268 is one size larger than the 258, and that it is still a non-CDL truck (under 26,000 GVW). The 268 has heavier springs, axels, brakes, and it has real truck tires. This model is a much better option for us.

For the tractor, important considerations are an air-ride cab, more than 300 horsepower, and minimal wheelbase to improve maneuverability in tight spaces. A wet kit on the tractor compares favorably to a pony motor for most users, and a rear differential lock is a nice to have. We operate with Kenworth T370s, and we like them; however, they do seem to have their fair share of false check-engine lights.

Container delivery and pick up is a collection of managed work. Your customer has to be informed and ready, the truck has to be in good operating condition, and your rental equipment must be in good shape to meet the customer's expectations. The truck's dispatch needs to be realistic and efficient, and the driver needs to get to the drop location and competently deliver the container to the ground. You as the owner need to oversee all that. It's work, but for us it all really helps us grow in our market.

Delivery Trailers

For many of us, our first delivery trailer was the little red wagon we had as kids. Pulling it around the yard, loading and unloading it, was a big deal for any kid. Now, my friends stop by our yard and look at the trucks, trailers, lifts, and containers and tell me that I own a grownup's playground. And they are correct!

Slide-Off or Roll-Back Trailers

Maybe the original and simplest type of trailer is a fixed flatbed. In this case, the container slides off the back end and hits the ground. Those who have used these know the risks and limitations. These trailers helped many of us get started in the business, but they caused a fair share of damage when boxes slid off the side instead of the back, or when they would not slide at all.

The more common and practical slide-off delivery trailer today is the tilt trailer that can either be a flatbed or gooseneck/ drop-deck style. The decks of these trailers tilt, lowering the tail and raising the front to facilitate a safe, smooth container delivery. In most designs, the tail of the trailer lowers to the ground as the front rises and the axles move forward. Although standard roll-off equipment trailers can work well, the container trailer is designed for the purpose. It has guiding rails, lighter GVW specs, container securing enhancements, and in some cases a chain-drive system instead of a cable winch.

With the flatbed style, the storage container will sit on the trailer over the truck's fifth wheel. With most designs, the bed slopes to the rear. Depending on the configuration, a high cube container could be over-height at the front. When the trailer tilts, most designs lift with the kingpin plate hinged to the trailer frame, raising the front of the bed. With the trailer axle in the forward position the rear edge of the trailer bed lowers to the ground and the container slides off.

The gooseneck-type tilt trailer allows the container to sit lower and flat on the trailer bed. The tilt of the trailer is achieved by a hinge between the trailer bed and the gooseneck. When the axles are in the forward position, the rear edge of the bed lowers to the ground. Compared to the flatbed style, the bed length is typically shorter, but the combined truck and trailer length is longer.

Side Lift

This type of trailer can lift the container off the trailer bed without tilting or sliding the container. Typical configurations pick up the container at the four bottom corners with hydraulic-controlled booms at each end of the container. These trailers are very specialized and cost more than their slide off cousins, but they can lift loaded containers, set containers on an adjacent flatbed, or even stack containers (depending on the model and design). The lift-off trailer can expand your business by offering loaded pick up, side pick up, loading of flatbeds, and "no tilt" delivery or pick up. There are also bobtail models available.

Image courtesy of Kiwi Container Lifting Services

Pickup Trucks and Fifth-Wheel Trailers

Over the last ten years, there has been a large increase in delivery truck and trailer combinations that are lighter duty than the traditional tractor-trailer. These are often called "hot shots." Some manufacturers offer trailers that can be used with just a three-quarter ton pickup truck. When this trend first began, there was a high incidence of equipment failures and (here in California) an inability for the highway patrol to classify the vehicle and trailer combination. Over time, the trucks have become more durable. We see many of them in service. A big plus for this arrangement is that most of the trucks are lighter and four-wheel drive reduces the chances of getting stuck in an off-road delivery.

Regardless of what delivery option you use, the "driver factor" is crucial. A perfect equipment delivery system can be rendered useless, or a poor-quality truck can be a money-maker depending on the driver. After several years of heavy driver turnover, we realized that to retain good drivers we had to pay well. Today, our average driver has worked for us more than four years. It's clear that the investment is well worth it. They work hard, customers like them, and they are paid well.

Living with the Risks of Operating Your Own Trucks

Years ago, I read that 75 percent of motorcycle accidents happen in intersections. From this we can conclude that motorcyclists would be well-served to avoid all intersections. But that is ridiculous. We can't avoid all risk. The best we can do is to know the risks we face and incorporate good business practices that mitigate potential impacts. Recently, one of my trucks swerved to miss a speeding driver in the slow lane as he was merging onto the freeway. It did not end well for us.

Considering the mileage we put on our five trucks, I assumed that an accident would happen sooner or later. But I was surprised by how I remained calm when I got the news about this event. There are several reasons why I could keep my composure. I was:

- *Realistic:* These things happen. We have not had an accident in recent memory. Statistically, we were on borrowed time!

- *Prepared:* After eighteen years in the business, we are not surprised when accidents happen. We take an objective view, avoid a heated response, and focus on any possible injuries. Thankfully, in this case, there were no injuries. Being prepared helps you turn a potential crisis into a mere mess that must be cleaned up. A large part of what we do is damage repair, so a mangled truck does not throw us into a tail spin. There is a profound sense of relief when there are no injuries and when the damage is limited to $150,000 worth of insured, rolling stock!
- *Compliant:* Because our drivers have complied with physical exams, CDL requirements, drug testing, and good driving records, we have no fear. Because our tractor-trailers have had the periodic inspections and recent inspections at the scales, we are in good shape. We also reduce worry by replacing tires before we need to. Because our tractor-trailers are less than two-years old, we know we have dependable equipment. This compliance stuff can seem like a waste of time and money. But when your truck has just wiped out sixty feet of freeway guard rail and a police officer tells your driver he was not at fault, you're glad you went through the pains of keeping your fleet in top condition and following the CDL rules for drivers.
- *Backed-up:* We have an extra truck and one extra trailer, plus a competent sub-hauler when we need him. We can't afford to run with one less truck, so we have to have back-up options when things go wrong.

In the accident mentioned above, the damage was not to people. If my truck had hit a car with a family inside, or if my driver had been injured, my writing here would have a much different tone. Two business friends of mine have had death-related accidents. I only observed a little of the impact, but it was profound. In one case, a trusted employee in a small company was killed on a job site. It was like losing a family member. All work stopped, and customers understood. They took time to grieve and to look after the deceased's family. It impacted the company in a solemn way.

The other friend leads a large paving company. An impaired driver slammed into his equipment at a night freeway repaving job and killed him instantly. The next morning there were news helicopters over the scene and reporters calling my friend's office. As a mid-sized company, they already had a plan for how to deal with this. Only one employee was allowed to talk to the press. The damaged paving equipment was pulled from the job site and held in storage in case it was needed as evidence. Jobsite staff were debriefed, and the safety manager collected all information related to the incident. It was an unfortunate accident, but the company had a plan.

Risk is often unavoidable. We cannot control much of what happens to and around us. But what we can control will have a big influence on the level of risk we face. Don't cross your fingers and hope for the best. Make plans for when bad things happen.

CHAPTER 4

Rental and Sale Equipment

PORTABLE STORAGE BUSINESS STARTS with a portable storage unit and is completed when a customer rents that unit. It seems simple, but choosing the right portable storage unit for your business and customer, and doing that multiple times is not easy. Understanding the issues of equipment supply, the types of equipment, the factors that influence supply availability, and the challenges faced by container manufacturers are all important. We'll start with availability ups and downs.

Predicting the Future of Container Prices

ANDERS NORLIN

Can we use fluctuations in the US dollar as an indicator for container prices? Over the last couple of years, container prices have fluctuated in an unusual way. What can we learn from these changes to make better purchasing decisions in the future? During 2001-2002, container prices were exceptionally low because of the worldwide recession. In 2003, prices started to inch up. Suddenly, in early 2004, they skyrocketed. We have all heard that the explanation is the super growth in China and carriers building larger ships, thereby needing more containers. I think there is an additional factor and that is the fluctuation in currencies. Furthermore, I think that we can look at the strength of our currency as an indicator for container prices. The constant oversupply of cargo containers in North America is a function of a trade imbalance, more merchandise being imported in cargo containers than merchandise being exported in cargo containers. Over time, there have been a few occasions with a reverse situation. The first was in the mid-1980s and more recently in 1995-1996, which was a period of equipment shortage and rising container prices following a period of a weak US dollar. During the early 1990s, the US dollar vs. the German mark (DEM), was around 1.70. In 1995, the DEM strengthened to around 1.35, a fluctuation of approximately 20 percent. It seems to me that there are three periods in the economic cycle that we should pay attention to.

The Strong US Dollar Period

During "good times" in North America, when we consume and import high volumes of capital goods, the US dollar seems to be strong and the equipment imbalance is large.

The Early Period of a Weakening US Dollar

When the consumption slows down and the US dollar weakens, there are still merchandise and containers in the pipeline based on the decisions made in the previous period. When the domestic economy slows down, local demand for containers declines and an over-supply is created, which means decreasing container prices.

The Late Period of a Weakening US Dollar

When the economy has slowed down, the demand for domestic containers is low, but an increase in demand for export containers occurs, which depletes the inventories in North America. In other words, the equipment flow is positive. Once there is a positive equipment flow, trading companies and direct sellers of container equipment are short of merchandise and prices start to rise. Therefore, the key is to make the purchases during the early period of a weakening US dollar.

Recent Trends

The charts below show the fluctuations of the US dollar vs. the euro and the fluctuation of the price for a 20-foot new ISO container over the last couple of years. Chart A shows a decline in the US dollar from the third quarter of 2003 through the fourth quarter of 2004. During 2005, the US dollar is strengthened, and during 2006 it starts to weaken again. Chart B shows that container prices have a reverse pattern. Prices are increasing from early 2003 through early 2005, dropping during the rest of 2005, and then climbing again in early 2006. Where were we in June 2006? Since the end of the first quarter of 2006, the US dollar has fallen 7 percent against the euro. Sticking to my theory that currency values are a leading indicator, we can see that in June 2006 we were in the first stage of the early period of a weakening US dollar. The dollar interest rates had increased substantially over the previous eighteen to twenty-four months, a factor that helped strengthen the dollar. The general expectation was that the cycle of rising interest rates for the dollar was coming to an end and that the interest rate for the euro would start to increase. Therefore, we were entering a period of a weaker dollar, which eventually led to fewer imports and more exports of merchandise in cargo containers. It would take twelve to fifteen months for these changes to take effect in the US domestic container market. At that time, we expected to see prices in June 2006 remain stable for twelve months, except for the seasonal fluctuations. During the first half of 2007, we saw container prices decrease.

Obviously, there are factors to consider other than the fluctuation of currencies, such as raw material prices, exceptional demand from wars, natural catastrophes, and structural changes in the industry. However, the strength of our currency is a projection of our economy, and that is important to consider when making investments in machinery and equipment.

A

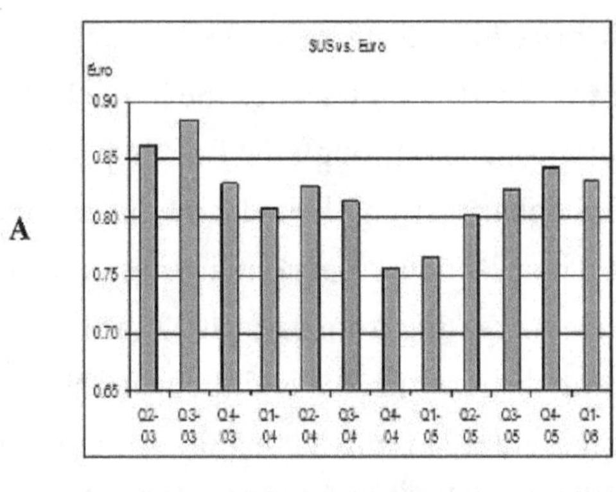

B

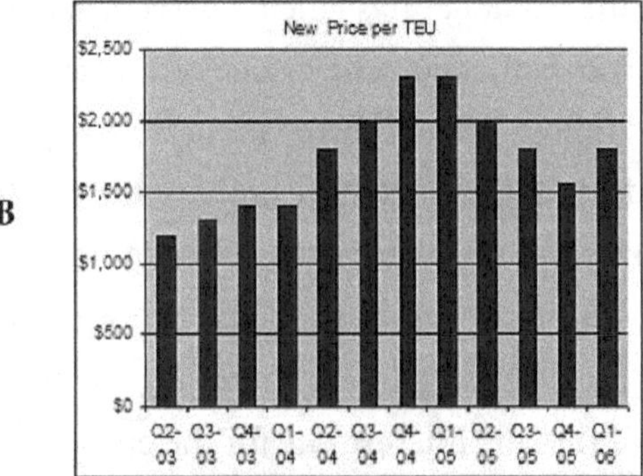

**The Euro was not used as a common currency in the 1990s; however, the German mark was often used as the key European currency since Germany is by far the largest industrial economy in Europe.*

Container Shortages and the Portable Storage Landscape

The shipping container industry saw a collective slump of 10 percent in 2009, the worst in the industry's fifty-four-year history. In the depths of 2009's downturn, one wondered how the companies would recoup their losses even in five years. Fortunately, that gloomy outlook dissipated, and the container shipping industry improved. So, did the leasing of maritime containers. Shipping lines were short on cash due to the downturn, but they had a strong future. The shipping companies filled their container needs by leasing containers from companies such as Textainer, Triton, Cronos, Florens, TAL Intl., CARU, and all the others that frequent our events.

The flipside for the portable storage and secondhand container industries was that the high demand for maritime container leasing led the shipping industry to hang on to the equipment longer, reposition more empties, and dedicate new production solely to increase the maritime container fleet. On top of that, "slow steaming" required more ships to service the same trade routes. Consequently, there was a need for even more containers. The shortage of containers for the maritime industry was equivalent to about two years of production. Furthermore, it didn't help that the container manufacturers had realized that they could manage financially without optimizing production by way of raising their prices.

As a result, the supply for the portable storage and secondhand container trading industry dried up rapidly during 2010 and the early part of 2011. Prices for containers increased. The peak season for the container shipping industry runs from June through October, as we all know. Typically, container inventories start to build up at the end of the holiday season, and in previous years, the resale departments of the maritime leasing companies start to ask their customers in the first half of January how many containers they planned to buy in the coming year. That's not something that happened in 2011. On the contrary, the shipping lines and container leasing companies tried to keep as many of their containers for maritime leasing as they possibly could. The supply situation in the United States was made even worse by a weak US dollar and high exports. This is something we welcomed from a national economic perspective, but not as we tried to make a living from buying, selling, and renting storage containers.

Companies operating in the portable storage industry can be impacted by various factors. First, those companies that are heavily dependent on trading will have a very tough time maintaining their businesses. With low inventories to trade, there will be low revenue, and if trading is the only activity, then there is almost no business. It is reasonable to expect that there will be a consolidation among the trading companies; the small undercapitalized trader will eventually run out of supply. As a pure trading company in the container industry, it is difficult to find alternative equipment to trade. One can get involved in reefer containers, tank containers and other specialty equipment, such as lifts and trailers, but this type of equipment requires more capital. More importantly, the technical knowledge that is required isn't easily acquired. Because this industry is transparent (the non-existence of exclusive distributorships and representations), there is no value in buying a small container trading company. Those that don't survive will have to wind down.

The medium-size trading companies that can take larger positions and add value to the equipment by making repairs and doing repositioning will do better. Keep in mind that there will still be damaged units, units in odd places, and other minor quantities available for sale from the shipping lines and maritime leasing companies.

In these situations, we usually see some smaller portable storage companies struggle as well. During the economic downturn, most of them seemed to have survived by reducing their rental fleets to generate cash. That cash was spent to pay for operating costs to allow the companies to stay alive. As the economy improved across the country, these companies were then faced with a situation in which they had neither cash to grow nor containers to grow. If the revenue from their rental fleets wasn't large enough for the companies to generate positive cash flow, they had to look at diversifying, which requires capital, or at divesting and exiting the industry.

Our industry giant, Mobile Mini, was at one point dealing with an extremely low utilization but was not selling many containers. The more pronounced a container shortage gets, the better this strategy seems work. Mobile Mini was ready to meet new demand when the economy improved. When a container supply situation is long-term, we can expect to see some smaller portable storage companies being offered for sale. These companies often lack the critical mass needed to generate positive cashflow from rental operations and they must rely on trading to support that cash shortage.

Now there are some bright spots. As container prices move up and supply is scarce, we'll see an opportunity to raise rental rates. Secondly, a company with cash-in-hand can purchase portable self-storage containers, such as the containers from PODS, 1800PackRat, Units, and others to diversify its fleet. These containers are more expensive than ISO containers, but the supply is reliable. You can place an order with any of the manufacturers and ten-to-twelve weeks later you have your shipment. With these types of containers in a fleet, a portable storage company can continue to grow in its existing market segment and expand into segments that don't want the more rigid ISO containers. In addition, for companies that have sufficient cashflow and that can maintain their existing rental fleets, there will be opportunities to acquire smaller local competitors. This leads to a larger market share and to more control of local rental rates.

When pricing portable storage rental fleets, operators are placing more and more emphasis on the yield that rental fleets generate. The prices for companies are set more on the basis of cash generated than a per-container value. It is at times difficult to comprehend how rental fleet pricing can decline while the container prices are going up. Theoretically, in a perfect market situation, a container on-rent should be worth as much as the sale container plus value added plus the amount of cash generated from an average rental term.

In our highly fragmented and erratically supplied industry, there is never a perfect market situation. Therefore, there is always an opportunity around the next corner.

Equipment Availability Cycles

PHIL HERNDON

There seems to always be an oversupply or undersupply of containers. Moreover, numerous factors and events can cause prices to increase or availability to dry up. You can be sure that when supply is low and demand is high that the factories will use every reason available to raise prices without admitting that demand is the cause. Conversely, it's always interesting to see that falling prices are never publicly attributed to anything. Here is a short list of events and factors that impact container pricing in China.

Material Cost/Supply

Steel is the largest expense in building a container, and steel prices can be volatile at times. When world steel demand increases, lifting steel prices, it's usually during a time of increased capital spending around the world, which also coincides with high demand for containers to move products. That is not a cycle for price stability. There was a time when Malaysia was unable to produce wood container flooring to meet production demand. This slowed container production and increased the price as available wood flooring became more expensive.

Global Trade

During the 2008 recession, as trade slowed to a crawl, the world's supply of containers began to pile up. There were reports of over one hundred idle ships with thousands of empty containers anchored in Singapore. Miles of unsold new containers lined the highways between the factories and Shanghai.

Upheaval in the Shipping Industry

In 2016, Hanjin, the seventh largest shipping line, went bankrupt. Tens of thousands of containers were stranded on ships that could not be moved or stacked in yards. Storage bills were left unpaid, and customers often had no direction on where to return the containers. All of this caused uncertainty and, for those who produced containers, an opportunity to raise prices.

Market Efficiency

With each passing year, shipping lines become more efficient with their inventory. The number of revenue trips per year a box makes has shown a steady increase each year. Consolidation of shipping lines and improved forecasting data have produced this result. Furthermore, consolidation of leasing companies also has given way to getting more with less. Idle inventory has been reduced to a minimum on all sides of the shipping equipment business, and this has impacted demand.

Arguably, we in the portable storage industry have no control over these factors, but it does help us understand the ups and downs of container pricing, both new and used.

When inventory is scarce, there are important factors for the local storage operator to consider. Some are good, and some are not.

- Fewer container sellers will be calling you.
- Those in your market who have available inventory will be able to seize market share.
- There will be pressure to increase rates.
- You may not be able to find containers to purchase, causing you to run short.
- The quality of used boxes in the market will decline significantly.
- Your gross sales may be lower.

Conventional wisdom would say that if you see the storm clouds of scarcity on the horizon you best stock up on inventory. I remember when 40-foot containers for sale on the wholesale market could not be found. Of course, I won a bid to supply fifty to one school district! As it worked out, I scrounged together as many 40-foot containers as I could, convinced the district to take 53-foot containers for the rest of the order, and finished okay.

Another consideration in times of scarcity is the decision to sell or rent. True, when sales prices are increasing, you can do well selling, but rental is always the better proposition. In most cases the container will still be rented even when supply problems have passed. Letting a competitor take your customer because you sold a box that you should have rented is poor business.

Then there is the oversupply condition. This occurs when a shipping line or leasing company demand slows and/or when global trade slows. It always seems as if inventory swells to ridiculous levels before the factories, leasing companies, and shipping lines begin to lower prices. I guess its misguided optimism. A slow reaction usually results in an overreaction. Like any market play, you can only guess the bottom; but usually the lowest selling prices occur when the oversupply has started to level off. Time is money, so it becomes a race among the suppliers to reduce unsold inventory.

Equipment Purchasing

As our rental fleets grow and we sell equipment, we need to purchase additional inventory. Success in purchasing equipment is dependent on numerous factors. We have all experienced the situation in which a price agreement was not fulfilled. When this happens in amounts well over $1000, these "misunderstandings" can be painful. So, the equipment buying process is worth talking about.

Timing

We have already talked about the macro-level economic factors that impact container prices and availability. Here we will deal more at the operators' level. But first some war stories.

It may be hard to believe, but the container supply market today is much more stable than it was in the 1990s and early 2000s. Once, I was offered a heavily discounted large number of 20-foot containers, but with no available cash I was not able to purchase any of them. Four months later, you could not buy a 20-foot container for five times that price! Around that same time, one of my suppliers wanted to get a large supply of boxes off the books, so he offered me a year-end special. I pulled the trigger and did very well.

Having funds to secure equipment at the right time in each market cycle is invaluable, especially if you have space to stockpile the inventory. Because shipping lines experience higher freight demand from June through November, sale equipment availability is typically scarce during that same period. For many of us in domestic portable storage businesses, that same summer and fall period is when we experience increased rental demand. But if you wait to add to your fleet in September, the equipment will usually cost more and be harder to find than if you had purchased in the spring. How do you find the balance of buying what you need without waiting too long and paying a premium for the equipment? Here are some ideas.

- *Develop solid vendor relationships.* Get close with two or three vendors and check with them regularly to confirm market trends, pricing, and availability. A good vendor can keep you informed and prevent you from over- or under-buying during changing equipment supply cycles. In exchange for that good service, be willing to do your part for the vendor. Don't nitpick about the condition of everything you buy. It is better to be a predictable and a positive buyer so that your supplier prefers you over your competitors. Be smart and pay your bills! Some people might enjoy the collections game, but most of us prefer a business relationship in which timely payments are something that happens without issue or question.
- *Know your own market cycles.* It's amazing, but some rental customers will rent from you seasonally every year. To serve them better, we developed a calendar to help us be ready. Regardless of how you do it, anticipating your customers'

needs will be critical in meeting the demands of your local rental market.

- *Remember that a good buy on the type of equipment you don't need is no buy at all.* There is nothing worse than missing rental opportunities because you don't have the equipment that your customers need. This will leave your yard stuffed with unrentable equipment.
- Maintain purchasing ability. If you have no cash or credit available to purchase equipment, you will be helpless to respond to the best opportunities to meet your inventory needs. But it's worse to ruin your reputation by buying something you can't pay for in a timely manner.

Location

Those of us near water ports or major transportation hubs can usually depend on adequate supplies of containers. For many inland locations, the availability of equipment can be spotty at best. Repositioning costs can also be a large part of your equipment purchase. For markets where boxes are normally scarce, you should probably buy based on local availability over need. I have a friend at a less-than-popular inland location and he aggressively buys anything and everything that comes into his area. While he benefits from not having to truck as much inventory to his location, his bigger win is keeping his costs lower than his competitors who must bring in containers from hundreds of miles away.

Condition

Often buyers will ask us the age of a container. Although age can be an indicator of condition, age is not a reliable measurement. We have seen five-year-old containers that looked much worse than fifteen-year-old equipment. Typically, 20-foot containers will have more wear and tear than vintage 40-foot containers. Some shipping lines do a better job of maintaining equipment than others. Brown (rust colored) containers always sell easier than gray or light-colored containers. If you have had a good experience with selling a certain series of containers, stay with that source as long as you can. It will pay off in the long term. Additionally if you have the ability to repair boxes, look for discounted damaged boxes. You can often find equipment that can be fully repaired with a couple of hours in your shop. Repaired boxes can be better than windproof and watertight boxes—at a fraction of the cost. Finally, every good sales yard has a box to show to customers who insist they want a lower price box, even if the quality is not great. Just don't buy too many of these sub-standard containers, because there aren't many volume buyers.

Terms of Sale

You can purchase equipment at another location and have it delivered to your location, or you can pay cash, or you can buy on credit. For more than twenty years, I have been buying and selling containers. Most transactions have been containers sold at a depot location with thirty-day payment terms.

Some suppliers offer equipment they do not own or control, and they expect payment in advance. This makes no sense at all. Why would you want to send money in advance to someone who does not have what you need? This has been an issue since the NPSA was founded. Members that send money ahead often find out there is a problem with equipment availability or release. Some have even heard the supplier blame *their* supplier! Avoid those situations.

If a company can't offer you any credit terms, ask yourself why not. You have an asset-based business that deals with a variety of vendors who are willing to provide thirty-day payment terms. So, a vendor who requires payment upfront could be suffering from poor cashflow, or possibly the vendor isn't able to meet the credit requirements of his suppliers. When you pay in advance, you are extending credit (or trust) to the vendor; so, it would seem reasonable to ask them for credit references!!

Just because someone is an NPSA member does not mean that they can be trusted or that they are required to operate their business as you might expect. The good news is that the NPSA has established a code of ethics. It enables members to file a complaint against an associate member who has not met that code. The code and complaint form can be found on the NPSA website. By filing a complaint, you are inviting the association's ethics committee to assist you in resolving your differences with a supplier.

I have advocated establishing a vendor certification program that would separate the suppliers who own or directly control sale equipment from those who do not. Your association leaders are aware of supplier problems and they are considering how best to deal with them. As in any business situation, buyers should beware; if a supplier is demanding money in advance, hopefully you can consider doing what I do: Call another supplier!

Value

Value comes in a variety of ways. The best price and the container's condition are critical factors. But remember that a $50 price difference can be forgotten in the first month's rent. Your relationship with an ongoing vendor can be strengthened when you see their needs and compromise a bit in a transaction. Value comes in the long term when both sides can build transactional trust. That is much more valuable than the best price you can find for a single container. Build trust with your vendors.

Take advantage of the association's benefits! When NPSA members attend industry events, we greet each other and smile! When buyers are smart about purchasing and vendors are smart about selling, we all benefit. Years ago, there was a container seller who was decked during a fight at an industry cocktail party (well before the NPSA started), but now the "Wild West" has been settled; we don't need cowboys and outlaws to do our business! We all can be professionals.

As the US Dollar Rises, Container Prices Decrease

ANDERS NORLIN

Typically, as the economy gets stronger, interest rates should rise. This means that loans will be more expensive, which results in fewer investments and slower growth. Depending on where you live in the country, you will have benefitted from the projected outcome. In addition, higher interest rates (or the expectation of higher interest rates) means a stronger US dollar, and that affects everyone in every economy that is dependent on the dollar, both here and abroad.

Most people in the US will look favorably on a stronger dollar. Perhaps this idea is built into our culture; we all want to pay less for vacations abroad. But it is a mixed blessing because a strong dollar isn't good for everyone. If you are an importer, you are happy because the cost of your merchandise is lower, and you have better margins without raising your prices. On the other hand, if you are an exporter, your products become more expensive for your customers in other countries with no benefit to you.

Changing Trade Patterns

A change in the value of the dollar will have an impact on cargo flow to and from the US. With a stronger dollar, we can expect imports to grow from countries that use the euro or other currencies. This in turn has an impact on container availability for portable storage companies. The inventories should increase, and the container prices should decrease. Imports from China normally don't change much because the Chinese yuan is, although no longer pegged to the US dollar, is controlled in a way that encourages stable trade. Since most US consumer products are shipped from China in containers, one shouldn't expect the container volume to change much on this trade route. If the dollar were to strengthen considerably, it is safe to say that we would see more containers available for sale at a lower price in North America. However, it would not be a glut.

Increased Sales Inventories in North America

Container leasing companies and shipping lines were looking to dispose of their containers built in the early 2000s—about two million TEU per year. With a strong dollar, there was a higher incentive to send sales inventory to the US and take advantage of the favorable currency exchange rates.

Declining New-Build Prices

There is often a decline in new-build container prices when there is an overcapacity and a slower economy in some parts of the world. Also, if prices go too low, the factories will stop producing, and that means there might not be any purchase opportunities. Never forget that everyone has to make money along the food chain (i.e. the factory, the middleman, the shipper, and the portable storage operator).

In summary, three factors often cause larger container inventories and lower container prices in the US:

- Growing imports and declining exports
- The efforts of container owners to direct sales inventories to the US
- Declining new-build prices in Asia.

Take Advantage of Lower New-Build Prices

With challenges come opportunities. When retail prices of storage containers aren't in sync with changes in new-build prices or second-hand wholesale prices in the short term, it can be a good opportunity for a portable storage operator to upgrade his or her fleet. Look over your fleet and see what you can sell at the retail level and what prices you can obtain. If those numbers are close to the cost of a new-build container, take advantage of this opportunity and start upgrading. A face-lift of your fleet now and then is not a bad idea. If you do it right, you could be able to sell units from your current rental fleet at higher prices than what you are paying for new-builds.

Secondly, if you expect your fleet to grow, take advantage of the lower prices and buy more than you need. Portable storage operators tend to be reactive rather than proactive. There is risk involved in taking on lower priced inventory that exceeds your immediate needs, but if you expect growth, you'll be able to rent out your expanded inventory with a higher margin than the containers you buy in the future. Remember, the future is always bright.

The Pitfalls of Creative Equipment Purchasing

PHIL HERNDON

Most single site operators have about four regular sources for purchasing containers: shipping lines, leasing companies, traders, and repositioning dealers. Each of these providers has its benefits and its limitations. Some do better when the market is flooded with containers and others when boxes are in short supply. Aside from these suppliers, there are others who sell containers. I discuss some of these companies and the challenges of buying from them.

First is the person with a box they don't need anymore. We get the calls and I am sure you do too. Most of these sellers are better salespeople than we are. "It's a solid box in great condition and easy to pick up. Just bring cash and the box is yours!" When and if we offer to buy these containers, we only do it after we have seen the container (pictures are okay), and only after we have negotiated a price that is typically 50 percent less than our regular suppliers. In the end, we usually sell the box at a discount and do our best to move them out as fast as possible. I see this as clean-up work, not a source of profit.

Another container seller is the thief. More than ten-years ago, someone I know in the business called to say he had some nice boxes for me at a competitive price. I accepted his offer and later that same day two near-new boxes came into the yard. I happened to recognize the shipping line, quickly called them, and confirmed that they were not selling the boxes. I immediately turned away those boxes. In another case, one of my friends once accepted stolen boxes. As a result, he had to sell his company to fund his legal defense. Although our industry has improved, all single-site operators should never take possession of a container without being able to easily confirm who the prior owner is.

The third seller is the container factory. I have two experiences and some observations regarding buying containers directly from the factory. But first I'd like to address when and why factories sell to single-site operators. They normally sell to leasing companies, shipping lines, and single-trip dealers. When the shipping lines and leasing companies stop buying, the factories dust-off their phone books and start calling anyone they see as a potential customer. It's happening these days. I recall that the last cycle like this was about eight years ago. When the big boys come back to put in five thousand unit-orders, the little guy's phone book will go back on the shelf.

My first experience happened about six years ago when four friends from around the country and I pooled funds and bought one hundred new 20-foot containers from a factory. We divided the country into five areas and agreed that if a box landed in one guy's area that person would buy it from the group. We all fronted equal portions of cash to make this happen. The distribution across the country worked okay. There were some bad damages and a few depot issues. Three months after we started, all but two boxes had been received. They took a year to tour parts of West Africa and were tough to sell as new once we received them. In the end, we all agreed it was a good experience, never to be repeated. The additional margin was not worth the additional work. It made more sense to buy single-trip boxes from dealers when and where we needed them.

In another situation, I was purchasing new reefers without cooling units through a US dealer for one of my customers in the US. After several transactions I began to purchase directly from the factory. My reason to go direct was cost and improved transaction efficiency. This was a big mistake. On each round, the price only went up and the factory always made changes to the specification and delivery date. These were small orders of six boxes. At one point, in frustration, I flew to Shanghai, took a three-hour car ride to the factory, had meetings, tours, dinner, and stayed overnight. Then I traveled back to Shanghai and never got a straight answer about the location of my containers! As things worked out, the boxes finally arrived, and the floors were inverted. My customer rejected them, and they were sold at a loss of more than $20,000.

In both cases I regretted that I dealt directly with the factory rather than a broker or trader who deals in higher volume. Had I done that, I would have avoided the issues that came up through the production and logistics processes. These experiences led me to appreciate the services these third-party brokers provide. I am sure that there are others who could share experiences that are different than mine, but for me the benefits of dealing with foreign container production could not outweigh the risks.

For those of us who have been in the container rental and resale business for more than twenty years, we see and understand the strength and stability represented through our current group of equipment suppliers. We value the service these suppliers give us, and we know we can depend on them though ups and downs. It's really no different than the way our customers depend on us!

Special Types of Equipment

I suppose the definition of "special equipment" could be anything that is not a conventional dry-cargo container. Over the years there have been variations within this group. We will only focus here on four categories of special equipment: flatracks, opentops, tank containers, and refrigerated containers. I offer this information not as gospel, but as my observation and experience from years of messing with this stuff.

Flatracks and Platforms

Flatracks (the generic name for this group) come in 20-foot and 40-foot lengths, and in the four basic configurations listed below. Units with end walls, when erected, are normally 8-feet 6-inches high. These units are used to move odd and oversized cargo that can be shipped while exposed to the elements. Heavy equipment, trucks, pipe, or oversized machinery are common commodities for this equipment. Here are the four basic types.

20-foot flatrack modified to carry a water treatment plant

- *Platform:* This configuration is just a simple flat deck. There are no fittings above the deck surface. Effectively, two steel I-beams extend the length with upper and lower corner castings (the corner piece on a container for lifting or locking containers together), and a wood deck with supporting cross members. This is the simplest variation of this group.

- *Flatrack:* The flatrack is a basic platform with the addition of fixed stanchions or end walls on each end. The stanchions include corner posts with headers that in some versions have an end panel between the posts and header. They are designed to be stackable. When cargo is loaded on the deck, a container can be stacked on top, as long as the cargo does not extend above the height of the corner posts.
- *Folding:* The folding flatrack has stanchions that fold inward. This allows the equipment to be moved empty in a compressed form. When the ends are folded down, a set of corner castings is exposed to allow for empty stacking.
- *Flush Folding:* This is the newest and most versatile type. The stanchions fold down like the folding, but with this design, they fold into the deck. So this unit can function like a flatrack or like a platform.

When purchasing these used, you should check the wood deck and steel cross-members as they are prime areas of deterioration. Additionally, many of these units were produced before Corten steel was widely used in container manufacturing, so rust can be a serious problem. When moving them, all but the conventional flatracks can be stacked for transporting. Weight and deck thickness varies widely between manufacturing series, so don't presume two racks are the same without doing a physical check.

In the resale market, flatracks are usually converted into bridges. The one drawback is that they are only 8-feet wide so it can be a little scary driving across a narrow bridge. I did that in a full-sized motorhome in northwest Arkansas once! Another use can be for creating portable processing plants. We have converted 20-foot racks for water treatment systems. In those cases, we placed 3/8-inch steel over the entire deck. The treatment equipment was mounted to that deck. Finally, a local customer used 40-foot platforms to move rebar to a construction site of several local bridges.

This is not a piece of equipment I would keep in sale inventory or one that I would add to my rental fleet. But if the need comes up, shop around a lot, because prices and conditions vary.

Opentops

These boxes come in 20-foot and 40-foot sizes and standard height. The design is basically a dry container with a canvas roof. Opentop components include the box itself (without a roof), a vinyl/canvas tarp, roof bows that support the tarp, and a cable that secures the perimeter of the canvas to the container (also known as a TIR cord). Most opentops have a removable header that swings out of the way so that odd-size cargo can be loaded. The width of the opening in the top may vary by an inch or two depending on the manufacturer.

Conversion opentops are dry containers that have been modified to function the same as a standard opentop. They have limitations on how long they can be used in service and they are typically certified for lower weight capacity than a regular opentop. The cost of these boxes is generally lower than that of a regular opentop. Also, the header over the doors does not swing away for loading like a purpose-built opentop.

Tarps are the item most often in need of repair or replacement. It's not unusual to replace a tarp on a ten-year-old box. Some of the larger depots stock tarps, but because the design of these tarps is specific to a manufacturer's production series. Tarps often must be made to order. There are several tarp suppliers. One that seems to have a good selection of templates is Martec in New Jersey. They can usually sew and ship a tarp within two weeks.

In the resale market, when buying a used opentop, it's critical to know your customer or market before you settle on a specific unit. An opentop with missing roof bows and a bad tarp is worth less than one that is ready to move cargo. However, that might be all you need for a resale opportunity. Confirming condition and completeness of the unit is always important. Also, an opentop with a missing or bad tarp may have a delaminated plywood floor since there are no drain holes in the floor.

Secondary uses of opentops most often include scrap or bulk material collection and transportation. Otherwise they are sold for one-way export shipments.

The two variations of opentops are half-high containers and hard-top containers. They are as their names indicate: half-high or built with a removable rigid roof, respectively. Application, design and resale issues are largely the same as with conventional opentops.

Tank Containers

There are a variety of specialized tanks used to carry specific liquids and gases. More popular in Europe than in the US, cargos range from wine to highly corrosive acids. Aftermarket uses include water or fuel storage. In my experience the cost to source this equipment will include significant repositioning expenses due to limited supply. Food-grade second-hand tanks will typically cost more than competing liquid storage solutions. As a result, this equipment is hardly worth considering in most resale opportunities.

Refrigerated Containers

Among the equipment types listed here, refrigerated containers are by far the most common, most widely used, and most readily available in water ports. The common sizes are 20-foot standard height and 40-foot HC. Since about 1992, standard height 40-foot containers have not been in regular production. Cooling units have been 440-volts and have used 134-amps, or an equivalent non-ozone depleting refrigerant. The cooling units are built separate from the container and mounted in a universal flange in the nose of the container, known as a picture frame. Thus, most cooling units are interchangeable with other containers.

The units operate on 440-volt, 3-phase electric power. Older units were 220-volt or capable of operating on either 220-volts or 440-volts. For the 440-volt only units, a step-up transformer is used for many domestic applications when 220-volt, 3-phase is the only power available. With a temperature range of minus 20 degrees up to a warm 80 degrees Fahrenheit, there is a wide variety of potential uses.

The most common cooling unit is made by Carrier, with ThermoKing and Daikin sharing a portion of the remaining market. The rugged service requirements, the wide temperature range, and the variety of cargo capabilities combine to make them expensive to operate as domestic storage. The cost of operation and maintenance is a factor that any domestic customer needs to understand. I do not recommend handling refrigerated container sales or rentals on a one-time basis. This equipment is best left in experienced hands because replacement parts can quickly exceed the replacement cost of the unit, and the value of ruined perishable goods can be staggering.

Nonworking units are in regular demand as insulated storage. They function very well for that purpose. One consideration to keep in mind is that the door seals do not allow for easy opening and closing of the container. Cutting off two of the three door seals will help.

When purchasing refrigerated containers, there are three primary considerations: age, condition, and cooling unit manufacturer. As mentioned earlier, purchasing, repairing, and operating this equipment is very specialized and may be better left to a supplier who has the required expertise. Recently, converted reefers have been offered as domestic-style cooling units for 20-foot containers. This equipment offers the benefit of new, simpler cooling units and reduced energy consumption.

For most of us, "specials" will never be a primary source of revenue. The demand is not consistent or significant enough to justify carrying the inventory. Nevertheless, having the basic product knowledge can help you be a better resource for your customers. As business would go, while writing this book, we did sell the 20-foot flatrack I bought four years ago because it was such a great deal!

Non-ISO Storage Equipment

In the last fifteen years, the portable storage industry has increasingly ventured into the use of non-ISO storage units, typically referred to as white boxes. These units tend to be attractive to residential customers looking for a storage unit that is less industrial than a shipping container used in domestic storage. In general, the white boxes are smooth walled, have easy-to-open roll or swing doors, and are less than 20-feet long. From an operator's viewpoint, they are not as durable as ISO boxes, but they can still be stacked (with each other) and delivered with a roll-off. They typically cost about the same as the mid-price point of a single-trip 20-foot container (the number between the short-supply cost and the oversupply cost).

Homeowners love the boxes because they look more like a PODS-type box, the doors open easier, and they feel cleaner. Since PODS pricing is so much more than typical portable storage rental, there is an opportunity with this type of storage unit, especially if there is a focused marketing effort. Also, white boxes are a reasonable way to construct a ministorage or to fill in the odd spots of a built-out ministorage.

Trailers

The use of semi-trailers as portable storage is nothing new, especially in the Midwest where containers used to be in short supply and trailers plentiful. Many NPSA members operate significant trailer fleets. Often cheaper than ISO containers, and many having roll doors that don't require space for door swing, there is a market for them. Also, anyone with a semi-tractor can move them. The downsides can include water leak potential, less security, and no ground-level access. But talking with a friend who owns some trailers, customers tend to rent them for longer periods, and the ability to move them loaded is a big feature.

Container Factories

As I write, we are in new cycle with the China container factories. Single-trip pricing is going up and availability is going down. After almost two years of relatively low pricing and plenty of inventory, this market swing could play heavy on box sales and rental fleet expansion. Without being the ultimate source of information on this, it seems appropriate to review the issues and potential impacts.

In a much-needed effort to improve China's air quality, the Chinese government mandated that all container factories switch from solvent-based to water-based coatings by April of this year. In my operation, we have used only water-based coatings for more than twelve years. We have found it to be relatively trouble-free, but we are not a container factory producing thousands of boxes. Here are some of the challenges.

- *Paint Curing:* Solvent-based coatings dry by evaporation. Solvent paints are surprisingly versatile, they cure fast regardless of the ambient temperature, and the solvents contribute to adhesion. Conversely, the curing of water-based paints is impacted by both temperature and humidity. Container factories in the North are heating the containers and the paint to get even marginal results. Factories in the South are dealing with high ambient humidity that causes rust bloom as the paint dries.
- *Application Equipment:* The factories are updating and replacing their paint systems to handle the new coating. The storage, handling, and application procedures are all being revised to accommodate this change, which is all expensive and reduces productivity.
- *Inspection and Warranty:* Typically, a container factory provides a three-year paint warranty. Seldom is there a paint failure during the warranty period. Independent inspectors certify proper coating thickness and coverage. There are already reports of large volumes of factory production failing paint inspections. The factories are more than a little worried about warranty issues and potential future paint failures and resulting claims.

- *Inventory Impact:* In anticipation of the paint change, demand spiked in the fourth quarter of 2016. Smart buyers saw the challenges of the coating change and the risk of 2017 being a low production year, not to mention the potential issues of quality and durability.

This change is like what occurred in 2001, when the refrigerated container industry switched from the miracle refrigerant R-12 to 134a. There was a steep learning curve and it put the industry on its ear for several years. The new refrigerant was not as versatile or efficient as R-12. Fleet conversion was problematic and there was panic, ignorance, wasted resources, and disruption as the industry sorted out the change. After some time, there was a return to normal operation, and the operators and suppliers survived.

So, with this coating change, what impact can the single-site operator expect?

First, higher prices. By most accounts, we can expect a 20 percent or higher increase. It seems that for years we have been experiencing price increase warnings followed by smaller than anticipated increases. But we also know that, on the retail sales side, any increase impacts sales volume because our customers are considering a variety of storage options.

Second, there will be less inventory to purchase. Since stocks have been cleaned out and factories are amid changing out spray equipment, we know there will be fewer incoming single-trip boxes. This will also put upward pressure on pricing and increase used container demand. It might be good to bulk up on inventory until this all sorts itself out. Otherwise you may find yourself with nothing to sell or rent!

Third, there are issues related to quality. Sometimes containers are like wine. There are less desirable vintages. A well-aged 2017 container built in northern China may not be a smart purchase. Untreated coating failure is something that gradually gets worse and is increasingly difficult to correct. Buyer beware!

Our industry can expect these types of challenges, but, ultimately, they are never as bad as expected. With good planning and flexibility, we can minimize the disruption to our operations. In fact, there are often opportunities to make money as these changes materialize.

Equipment Supply

Because portable storage is not a fully standardized industry, and because our customers use our services for many purposes, the storage unit can be made of almost anything—if it meets the customer's typical needs, and that it is safe, accessible, secure, durable, transportable, and dry. It would be fascinating to consider the impact of a new equipment design on container shipping and leasing companies. What if there were a better-suited design for our purposes than the good old-fashioned, near-bulletproof 20-foot container. Who knows? We live in a fast-changing world. The possibility of such a replacement is something to watch for.

CHAPTER 5

Marketing

Marketing in the Public Storage Industry

PHIL HERNDON

I often meet people who want to start their own business, and my question is always the same: Who is your customer and how are you going to get them to use your service? Marketing is how you get your customers. Of course, how you keep them is important, but if you can never get the customer in the first place it's a moot point!

This chapter is arguably the most important one in this book. To be honest, it could also be the most lacking! Marketing is a wild card. It's always changing, it requires you to duck and weave, it's subject to copycat competitors, and it never lets you rest. So, as you read this chapter, remember that marketing is a moving target.

Free Advertising

How many businesses will pay you to put your billboard on their property? Well, a portable storage business will. So, it pays to invest in your fleet's appearance. We take it very seriously. If our box is sitting next to a competitor's, we want ours to make his look old and tired!

It starts with a good coat of paint. We have tried several types of paint and have found a product that requires minimal surface preparation, is easy to apply, and has resistance to weather and fad-ing. The paint is a water-based DTM (direct-to-metal) paint made by a local industrial paint supplier. We use a semi-gloss, costing less than $20 per gallon. Don't forget that flat gray starts to look like primer real fast. The chapter on operations goes into more detail about paint and painting a container. If you are in a pinch, we've heard that Walmart's deck paint applies well on containers, stands up to the elements, and is cheap; just remember that it is not direct-to-metal, so any exposed metal will need to be primed before the top coat is applied.

Decals set you apart. We believe our decals must be:

- *Large enough to read* from 100-feet away and have our 1-800 number up high on the sidewall. Often the container is behind a fence or in a blocked area. We want the potential customer who sees our container to pick up his cell phone and call us! It helps if he or she can do that without going on a safari to find out who we are.
- *Colorful and attractive.* I know a rental company that puts a smiley face (yellow circle with a smile on it) just as a way to perk up their rental fleet. People call and ask, "Are you the company with the smiley face on your containers?" It pays to be attractive!
- *Distinctive.* Those who don't have a gray fleet probably have a beige fleet. They all really look the same. Although none of us wants to build a business with pink containers, we all struggle to be distinctive. Our approach is to put an extra decal on the side. It says, "Check us out on the web," with our website URL placed below that. Maybe you have a local or community cause that your container can support. Be creative.

You should be able to find some excellent choices for decal suppliers in your area. Several years ago, I asked four friends from different parts of the country to provide pricing for their local decal suppliers. We discovered that the prices were all close to each other. For our containers, we have two side decals at 4-feet tall and 2-feet wide, and a couple of small decals that run diagonally in the corners for a cost of $55 per unit. We used to have a multicolored graphic of an elephant stuffed into a container. That became a real challenge. My local supplier, with reservation, agreed to supply these. After six months of UV exposure, the decals faded. Thankfully, last year at the annual NPSA conference, I explained my experience to an NPSA associate member who supplies decals and he was able to provide what I needed, with UV resistance, at a competitive price (thanks NPSA!!). The new elephant goes over the old and our distinctive image is preserved.

Regardless of what color containers or decal scheme you choose, your container is a billboard that visually sells your service. Unit appearance may be your cheapest and most effective form of advertising. Don't neglect it.

Getting the Phone to Ring

The American Marketing Association defines marketing as, "The process of planning and executing the conception, pricing, promotion, and distribution of ideas, goods, and services to create exchanges that satisfy individual and organizational goals." But I'm a simple guy in a simple business, so my definition of marketing is: "What makes the phone ring?" We see that as our number one business objective.

I went out to some portable storage operators and asked them what they did to get their phone to ring. The responses, although almost random, indicated that there is no set formula for the way to attract customers. But I will try to summarize what I heard and learned, and I'll inject my own observations.

Response 1: "Place your physical operation in a highly visible location with banners on containers. Include your phone number, the words 'Containers for Rent,' and your company name." Over the years I have talked to several operators who indicate this is a key element to marketing. If the customer can see you, they will call you. Although I like that idea, here in California visibility can also draw the wrong attention; inspectors from every government agency imaginable, plus vandals. But I'll keep this in mind when my yard lease is up in eight years. Maybe I'll be able to afford a better location by then!

Response 2: "Place huge decals on the sides and ends of every container, even sale boxes!" I agree with this, as noted before; it's free advertising. So, we reviewed our decal scheme and we are looking to add decals to our doors. We will also move our sidewall decals more to the center so that they can be seen even when a door is open. Although I am not willing to supersize our decals, I do agree we could do more in this area.

Response 3: "Use bulk mailing to specific SIC codes followed by phone calls to that group." This company uses a mailing service. Two weeks after the postcards go out, they have everybody in the office go to the phones and call each potential customer on that list to offer their service. They can track the surges in on-hires that result from these campaigns, so they know that it works. I have considered this strategy in the past, but I have yet to put something together. Customer cold calling is not what I return early from lunch to do, but if the evidence is there, this may warrant some consideration.

Response 4: "Visit every new rental customer." The operator who offered that advice has a large fleet, so to hear this from him caught me by surprise. But then I started to think through this; if we add on average eight new customers per month, that is only two visits per week. I could do that on my way home! In fact, if I did this, I might learn more about what my customers need. That knowledge would prepare us to adjust and meet future challenges. I really like this idea. But I learned about it a month ago, and I have yet to visit a customer!

Response 5: "Let your good service speak for itself and then be patient." If you listed my attributes, the list would be short, and it would not include patience. I'll have to delegate this one! But I strongly believe in letting good service speak for itself. We constantly receive referrals and are regularly gratified by kind words from past rental customers who share about us to potential rental customers. It is a lot better to build strong customer relationships with positive people who value service than to cut prices to beat our competition. Single-site operators know that good customers look for competent business relationships, and that's good because we do our work with pride and dedication.

Follow-up is critical to the subject of marketing. If you don't measure the response, you will never know what avenue leads to the best return. Our office staff agrees that asking, "How did you hear about us?" is a simple way to make the phone ring. We do it sometimes, but not all the time. So much for good intentions!

I want to thank my friends who gave me valuable insights into marketing. I also want to leave this door open for discussion. All of us need to challenge the notions of what we do and why. We need to open our eyes and ears to our market and ask how we can attract the customers we want and need. Only then can we accomplish our goal of building a strong business that represents us well in our community.

Internet Marketing

I think I was forty-years old before I had a computer, and I remember watching in amazement as a fax machine spit out a ship stow plan as my pager reminded me to call my boss! The last twenty years have been revolutionary with respect to the dissemination and use of information. An NPSA member in our single-site forum shared a website that offers ramps for container access. I checked it out and for the last three days I have been seeing ads all over my screen for container ramps! It's a little unnerving!

Most of us have a website and many NPSA members use pay-for-clicks advertising. This service lets you select key search words and, for a fee, your website is presented to Internet searchers who use your keywords. I hesitate to write this, because all this is changing so fast. Ink is hardly dry before a new thing renders the old thing useless!

We have hired a company (an NPSA associate member) that works to optimize our web presence, customer connections, and keywords. They provide a system that tracks searches, captures customer phone and Internet contacts, and gives us data that shows the effectiveness of our "campaign." Simply stated, it works. Our call efficiency is notably improved, and the conversion data will make it only better in time.

I remember long ago receiving calls from people saying things like, "Is this the Container Store," or, "Do you sell Tupperware containers?" So, I really appreciate the Internet as a marketing tool!

Marketing Masters?

One of the most remarkable changes in the storage industry over the last ten years has been how PODS single handedly created an industry and identity squarely between the portable storage and ministorage segments of the market. This resulting rise of PODS-type operators has created a fundamental shift in our business. The portable storage operator would do well to learn from PODS.

What has PODS taught us?

They taught us that marketing can trump price. We are constantly amazed that customers will call us for a rental rate and be in shock at how much cheaper we are than the PODS basic service. How can we be so much cheaper? (Or as some would say, why can't we charge more?) The answer is that a marketing driven perception has programed consumers to believe that PODS provides a better product. PODS has created an image of a clean storage unit, delivered by clean trucks and customer friendly drivers. My company does the same, but I have not spent millions getting that word out to potential customers.

They taught us that there is a retail side to our business. Since its beginnings, the portable storage business has focused on business-to-business relationships. Over the years, I have talked to several operators who would not rent to a private party. Only in the last year or two has Mobile Mini identified private parties as a business focus. But it can be difficult to shift gears from our usual business customers to work with an individual customer who is trying to decide if their furniture will fit in a 20-foot container or if they should order a 24-foot box instead. Nevertheless, PODS has done very well at handling private parties and keeping them happy. We can learn from them.

They taught us that customers want clean storage units. My neighbors rented a PODS unit and it sat in my view for four months while they remodeled their home. I asked why they didn't use me, and I was bluntly told that my containers are not clean enough! In truth, my containers *are* clean enough. I suppose I could shoulder the blame for not getting that message out. In fact, PODS has capitalized on our silence in this area. They've worked to establish the benefits of their units over containers and steel storage units. Maybe it's time we institute a policy that all rentals to private parties be steam cleaned before delivery? I have an air freshener that we seldom use. Maybe that would be a good thing also.

They taught us that there is a demand for moving and storing loaded storage units. Years ago, the boundary of our business was understood: We are neither a mini-storage nor a moving and storage company; we simply deliver and pick up empty containers. Maybe it's time to change that. With most US markets served by loaded container lifters, it seems we should be able to provide a moving option without a major investment. We have done a couple of simple loaded moves recently and we've benefited from the revenue, the expanded relationships, and the extended rental periods.

They taught us that our business can be franchised. Most of us have grown our businesses through a set of policies and procedures that keep things running profitably and smoothly. For years, container leasing companies dabbled unsuccessfully in franchise-type relationships with domestic container rental companies. Even Mobile Mini, in the early years, started with and then stepped away from a franchise network. A franchise offers a combination of professional disciplines and onsite owner presence. While most of us would have no intention of becoming a franchisee, we do need to recognize the long-term benefit of running our businesses in a professional and standardized manner that creates a predictable customer experience year in and year out.

They taught us that storage security may not be as critical as we thought. Many of us tend to brag about how secure our containers are, but it's a fact that most of us are offering a product designed to carry 30 tons of cargo when customers sometimes just need to hold a lawn mower and some power tools. But our containers are secure, and they can take a beating. Meanwhile we see these plastic, plywood, or light-metal units used by PODS and wonder how a customer can feel secure using them. I am not suggesting that we downgrade our equipment, but I am suggesting that we look for ways to remind customers about the importance of security without focusing on the overbuilt nature of our equipment.

PODS has not taken all the business and left us with the scraps. In fact, I would say the opposite; their marketing has taught us a lot about our customers, what they want, and how to get a message to them. Additionally, they have taught the consuming public that there is a better way to store belongings. This new, broader group of customers insures our future if we choose to capitalize on the opportunity.

Networking: A Marketing Event or Just Being Yourself?

ANDERS NORLIN

If you are a member of NPSA, you have most likely gone to one or more of the organization's events that take place in various cities around the country. Each place has something unique to offer.

It's natural to want to go to interesting places, but when you come to one of NPSA's conferences, you come to visit the NPSA and to network. The conferences have educational programs during which all of us learn something. But the main reason we take part in the conferences is for the networking opportunities, to meet and talk with industry peers and to learn how operators run their businesses.

Networking is about more than going to industry events; it is also a part of your regular life. Your relationships with family, friends, and professional colleagues can be as valuable to you as the relationships you establish within industry groups. Some people are more adept at networking than others. It is a very personal skill. Extroverts do better than introverts. Younger people often do better than older people, and women generally do better than men.

Networking is very important for any business owner's success, so let's talk about how you can improve your networking skills.

- *Make it fun:* You don't make new contacts if you are not in a positive mood.
- *Show up:* Being present at many events shows your commitment.
- *Listen:* It's amazing how people appreciate being listened to.
- *Be engaged:* Show your sincere interest in people's businesses and lives.
- *Be generous:* Give something to those you meet rather than asking for something.
- *Take initiative:* People gravitate to those who want to do things.
- *Keep it up:* Maintaining relationships means staying in touch on a regular basis.
- *Be patient:* It takes time to see the benefits of networking.

This list of simple ways to improve networking effectiveness isn't that complicated, so go and do it. If you feel that your networking skills need improvement, you have started the process, and that's good!

Plan Your Networking

Figure out how you can network while maintaining your busy schedule. First, divide networking into categories; for example, professional, family, and friends. Take a look at your calendar and categorize your upcoming events within these groups. If there is too much of one category, try to find a balance between the three. Think of what you expect to experience from each of your upcoming events. If some of the events seem a bit uninteresting, take the initiative to make them interesting by contributing something that takes the event in the direction you want it to go while still providing good content to others.

Become Part of the Group

People like to do things with people they like, but it is a challenge to be new to a group. Some individuals enter new groups very easily, usually because they understand how people function within the group. So, when you meet people, ask them simple questions or start some small talk to get a conversation going. Once you have opened the door, try to figure out the topic of greatest interest. In a business environment, it is always safe to ask what a person does. Most business owners like to talk about their business accomplishments. Listen to them and learn. Give them some information of interest. Soon you will have added a new person to your network.

Social Networking

Facebook, LinkedIn, and other social media platforms can be useful networking tools, but they take some skill. I use Facebook for family and friends, and LinkedIn for business relations. A few people in my network overlap both platforms; after all, we do make good friends from business contacts now and then. I do not connect with people I haven't met. Some event participants will send you connection requests, but you have to draw a line somewhere. Facebook and LinkedIn are good tools for networking, but I make sure to contribute value to my connections. Therefore, I am selective about who I connect with on either site.

Expand Your Social Networking

Establish a plan for who you want to connect with and give yourself a timeslot every day for networking. Set a goal for new connections on a daily, weekly, or monthly basis. As you do this, make sure you send information of interest to your existing connections on a frequent basis. You don't want to be "unfriended" due to a lack of activity.

In summary, networking is a good business practice. It requires engagement, involvement, and effort. If you work with a friendly, useful, and genuine approach, you will see benefits in the future.

Network Marketing

PHIL HERNDON

As a refugee from a large corporation that was self-sufficient and independent in our market, my colleagues and I never learned the value of developing relationships with others in my industry. We acted like we had some secret that, if it were revealed, might negatively impact our market share. Now after more than twenty years in business, my viewpoint has changed 180 degrees. I am an open book. I won't email you my customer list, but I regularly share how our business is doing. I am confident that this openness has helped us grow and improved the quality of service we provide our customers. I credit the NPSA for establishing the platform that helped me make this change.

Define the change? Two concepts come to mind. The first is "reciprocity" and the second is "word of mouth." Reciprocity, in social psychology, refers to responding to a positive action with another positive action, rewarding kind actions.

Thanks to the Internet, we receive several calls from people seeking equipment outside our service area. Once we determine their location, we refer them to someone else in the association. This is not a big deal and we don't ask for anything in return. We see and know the benefits of helping, and we welcome the opportunity to refer customers.

There are still a few who want to rent a container from us so they can rent it to someone in our area. As a rule, we discourage this practice; it is contrary to the focus of our business. Early this year, we mistakenly rented a container to someone who rented it to an out-of-state contractor with a job in our service area. Last week, the contractor called us and explained that he had called for an off-hire three-months earlier. He said the box had not been picked up and that he was still getting billed for it. Once I explained that there was a broker between us, he was livid. I encouraged him to call me next time he needed a rental box, adding that I would introduce him to a local NPSA member near his next job.

The receiving part of reciprocity can only happen when we give first. Twenty-years ago, some people in the rental business looked for ways to avoid reciprocity. They would offer a referral opportunity in exchange for a portion of revenue or other compensation. I tried several of these approaches and none were successful. If you consistently refer customers, your generosity will come back to help you.

Word of mouth, according to Mark Zuckerberg, CEO of Facebook is: "People influence people. Nothing influences people more than a recommendation from a trusted friend. A trusted referral influences people more than the best broadcast message."

As the years pass, NPSA members know each other better. As a result, our opportunities to upgrade a referral increases. Simply sharing a phone number for service in another location can be transformed into a personal recommendation. When I tell a customer, who is asking for a rental box in Seattle, that I have a friend there who is a member of the NPSA and a great guy, my referral becomes personal. It's a proven fact, as Zuckerberg stated, that personal referrals are the most trusted form of marketing. Each year, as I attend NPSA events, and as I communicate with other members between meetings, I see the value of sharing information and supporting other NPSA colleagues. Yesterday we finished a project that I shared with a half dozen industry friends. If a customer calls one of those friends asking for a container in my area, my friends will recommend me and vouch for my work. The networking becomes personal. That is when a referral becomes "word of mouth." The big guys with staff changes, reorganizations, training manuals, and centralized customer service departments can't compete at this level.

Relationships you have developed through the NPSA to share and receive leads could be the largest single benefit the association provides. Transforming those shared leads into word-of-mouth referrals is up to you, but doing so might be the second largest benefit the NPSA provides!

When I was in business school, my marketing class teacher was an expert on champagne. We finished the course as experts in champagne marketing! Although there are universal elements to marketing different products, marketing is always changing. No single program will ensure long-term success. If marketing is constantly changing, we should also be willing to change and grow.

How to Make Sound Marketing Investments

ANDERS NORLIN

We all spend money on marketing. There are several ways to measure the results. However, the effects of marketing are difficult to measure with *accuracy.* The first challenge is that only some marketing efforts can be measured effectively. The second challenge is related to the timing of when to measure the outcomes.

Identify Measurable Marketing Programs

The first step in the process of measuring the return on your marketing investment is to identify the specific marketing programs that can be measured effectively. These are called the Measurable Marketing Programs (MMPs). Start by looking at your sales and break out the amounts that can be attributed to specific marketing efforts and those that can't, which are called Immeasurable Marketing Programs (IMPs). MMPs include web traffic, click rates, email opens, coupons, telemarketing, TV commercials, exhibiting at tradeshows, and others. IMPs include media presence, sponsorships, billboards, visiting trade shows, customer referrals, etc.

Residual effects of past MMPs fall under this category as well. In other words, sales from past marketing efforts are not something that can be efficiently measured. This process helps you focus on marketing activities that can be measured and from which meaningful measurements can be obtained.

Measurements for Marketing Programs

Once you have established the MMP, look at your data and establish what is meaningful for you. Spreadsheets are the most obvious ways of looking at numbers. For example, if you exhibited at a trade show that cost $10,000 and you made two hundred new contacts at the show of which ten ordered your product at a price of $2,000 each, then each new contact cost you $1,000 and generated $1,000 in net revenue. In traditional financing, the return on Investment (ROI) from this marketing activity is 100 percent.

The challenge with this method is determining how much revenue you got from visitors that you met last year and how much revenue you got from those who saw your name on the list of exhibitors but never visited your booth. Neither of those questions can be answered with accuracy; therefore, we have to use another measurement. An alternative method is the Revenue-to-Cost Ratio (RCR), which takes the incremental revenue from a marketing event in relation to the cost of the event. In our example the RCR is 200 percent.

The Timing of Measuring a Marketing Program

In the portable storage industry, we know that a customer only rents a container when he or she needs one. We can't time our advertising to match that specific moment. Therefore, it is important to have measurable marketing programs, otherwise you run the risk of marketing to an audience that isn't listening. One method is to track all marketing activities and time them with sales revenue. A good way to start is with a simple graph showing monthly revenues and the costs of different marketing activities. If you stay disciplined and do this year after year, you will see patterns from which you can make meaningful decisions.

Once you understand what a marketing activity does for you, it becomes easy to start ranking marketing decisions. Should I advertise in the newspaper? Should I pay to do telemarketing? Should I have a Google pay-per-click campaign, etc.?

Measurements of Social Media Marketing

We associate social media with fun more than business; however, there are some social media measurements to include in your analysis. Social Media can help you stay in touch via electronic media, but as you consider the list of social media measurements below, be sure to remember offline communication too. The good old phone call or a cup of coffee with a customer are good examples.

- *Prospect Engagement:* Prospects, clients, and customers are engaging online via social media; measure the feedback from contacting prospects.
- *Prospect Virility Score:* Prospects are active online; measure the referrals and the "likes" to establish the validity of your social media marketing efforts.
- *Search Engine Ranking ROI:* When customers consider buying products or services, they go to online services. Measure your search engine ranking.

Establish a method to measure the use of your social media tools and include those numbers in your analysis.

Conclusion

It is difficult to effectively measure the ROI in marketing programs; some programs *can't* even be measured. The measurements vary from ROI methods to those based on total sales. Build a history and compare long-term revenues and costs and establish patterns that can be meaningful for decision-making. Learn how to measure the effects of social media.

Finally, the numbers from different measurements will help you make decisions; however, they should be combined with the personal input of the operator. The numbers only show history. Although they may show trends in your world today, they should supplement the input from someone who has a feel for the market and the business environment. Therefore, listening, talking, reading, and investigating are wise ways to make financially sound marketing decisions.

CHAPTER 6

Staffing

I (Phil) deeply appreciate the value of the people who work for us. I want those who work for us to be better people for the experience. Cared-for employees know how to take care of customers, fulfill their responsibilities, and challenge their fellow employees. They are instruments that play the song you feed them, so why not make that song the best it can be?

One of my employees recently challenged my approach (in a healthy way) to an operational matter. I appreciate it when employees see ways for our company to improve. It also winds my clock to hear from customers who say our drivers are the best in the business. I'm happy when one of our mechanics takes enough pride in his work to haul me from my desk to the shop so I can see what he's accomplished. Employees are the lifeblood of your company!

A typical rental company with a fleet of two hundred units on-rent will have one owner, one sales/collections person, one driver, and, if there are enough sales, a full-time shop person. When a rental fleet has four hundred units on-rent and the monthly sales revenue is about equal to the rental revenue, you can usually double the staffing listed above. Currently, we employ fourteen people. I never want to miss a rental opportunity, so we stay a little fat on drivers to cover those need-it-right-now opportunities!

Employee Education

ANDERS NORLIN

Large corporations can spend enormous amounts of money on education and employee training programs. Typically, the family-owned portable storage company does not do that, despite the importance of ongoing training and development.

It is vital that employees continue to learn. Providing education is another way to retain talented employees. Although most employees go to work to make a living, those with drive and ambition also want to get to the next level in their careers. If you provide meaningful education and training for your employees, you foster engagement in the business. If the employees know they can move up the ladder or enrich themselves through education, they will be more enthusiastic about the company and the company's progress.

What Do You Teach Your Employees?

There are many educational programs a company can purchase, including courses related to HR, accounting, and safety. But I recommend that you start with the basics of your business. Look at the key numbers of your company. How do you, as the owner, measure success? Portable storage container rental is a simple business. Therefore, teach the employees to understand the following key numbers.

- How many containers are on-rent?
- What is your average rental rate?
- Which customers aren't paying us?
- What is the average delivery distance?
- What is the average delivery cost?

Display Vital Business Information

I visit many companies in the industry and often suggest that simple data should be displayed for everyone to see. Regardless of whether it is the owner, the accountant, the mechanic, or the driver, all staff should know how the business is doing and what is changing. If you post key data on a regular basis and discuss it with your employees, you will receive more engagement, input, and suggestions from them.

Give Employees Instruction that Matters to Them

We live in a fast-moving world. The average person has a complicated life. People often don't understand how to evaluate the many options they have. Therefore, teach your employees about things that matter to them. For example: how to best finance a car purchase; how life insurance works; what are today's health insurance options; how to improve credit ratings.

Allow Employees Time for Education

Show your employees that you are committed to educate them, but make sure they know you expect from them a commitment to learn. Time is of the essence. Everyone expects that company education is on company time. To show employee commitment, split educational time between personal time and working hours. For example, if your work day ends at 4:30 p.m., have the education sessions between 4 p.m. and 5 p.m. Half on company time and half on personal time.

Show the Owner's Commitment to Education

In most small owner-operated businesses, everyone looks to the owner for guidance. Therefore, take charge of educational sessions by being present. If you know the subject, be the instructor. If you mix it up by bringing in professionals to teach subjects beyond your expertise, then your employees will respect you.

Listen, Listen, and Listen

Listen to what your employees have to say during educational sessions. You will learn a lot about what matters to them. You can use the information to improve your business. During educational courses, employees can express concerns without being in the boss-employee situation. They might not speak frankly, but you will understand which questions are related to the business and which are not.

Certification

Many companies need people with various types of certification. When you give your employees time for certifiable education, encourage them to take courses outside your business. You may lose some employee time, but they will be exposed to new views and ideas that can benefit the company.

Formal Education

Many young adults go to college because they are told it is the thing to do, but many never finish because they lacked a goal. A few years in the working world can help people formalize their goals and give them a reason to finish their education. Show your commitment to those employees by offering them time to study, or by contributing to their tuition. By doing this, you will build loyalty and commitment among your staff, and you will benefit from having employees with knowledge of the latest from the academic world.

Rewarding Employees: Do I Really Have To?

PHIL HERNDON

At an annual NPSA conference in November 2016, in Las Vegas, as part of the operators' roundtable, I spent time with owners talking about how to reward our employees. The discussion was nothing less than enlightening. Around the room, owners shared how they rewarded and motivated their employees (or failed). I'll share here some of my thoughts from that session.

Don't get stuck in a reward rut! One owner shared how each year his company had a reward event. He observed that it didn't seem like a reward to the employees. After three years of receiving hams and bottles of wine, employees came to expect the "rewards." Families began to plan the Christmas meal around that ham! So, add diversity to the way you reward your employees.

Next, make your rewards personal. Years ago, when I worked for APL, we went through a "committee" season. It was demoralizing. We stopped being individuals. Everything was done in committees. As a result, good ideas and creative thoughts were lost in endless committee meetings that produced average results. So, find ways to reward your top employees in personal ways, both publicly and privately. Those people will set the standard for the rest of your staff.

Keep the big picture in mind. If you set strategic yearly goals for each of your business segments, don't hide them from your staff. Regularly remind employees of the company goals. That will help them connect business decisions to the goals. For example, you might say, "We are doing this because we set a goal to improve sales by 10 percent." Most owners are the originators, communicators, and leaders for strategic goals, so keep your rewards in line with those goals.

Create programs that foster a team focus. In my company, we had an off-the-chart May of 2013. All of us worked hard and together to attain that result. As the month progressed, it was cool to watch my shop guys get excited about producing more rental boxes. We all could see and feel the growth. At the end of the month, on a Friday, I thanked each employee (individually) for the effort and handed them a $100 bill. The $100 wasn't much, but my sincere thanks and our collective celebration meant a lot to them.

Although I'm not great at this, spontaneity is important. In general, my creative side runs at a deficit when it comes to spontaneously rewarding people. Writing this book helps me be more disciplined in areas that I might not be good at naturally. So, if you are like me and tend to rationalize why you shouldn't give a $10 Starbucks gift card to each of your drivers after a demanding week, suppress your rational side and buy the gift cards. Let them know you appreciate their work!

Also do whatever you can to foster pride. Last year I bought company logo shirts for everybody. I was surprised by the response. We took pride in how we looked and the way we presented the company. The shop guys refused to wear their shirts in the shop, but they wear them walking to the locker room. They would not dream of getting them dirty while repairing a container! We have since added jackets and hats. The cost of the attire was insignificant, but the pride in wearing the name and logo has benefited the company and the employees.

All this requires you, the owner, to pull away from seemingly bigger issues and become creative! There was a person at a NPSA annual conference who had worked for the same company for eighteen years. She was quick to praise the unique ability that her boss had in giving the right thing and at the right time. Her boss's leadership skill moved her from an entry-level position into a partnership role. It is worth it to invest in employees!

Organizational Culture, Programs for Unison Value, and Company Directions

ANDERS NORLIN

Do your employees know where you want to take the company and are they all going in that direction? Many portable storage companies are family-owned and operated. Family members know each other and understand how each individual thinks and behaves. This is known as "the organizational culture." Organizational culture is the behavior of humans who are part of an organization and the meanings that the people attach to their actions.

Once the owner-operated company starts to grow and non-family members are hired, the new employees need to understand the organizational culture. The "family way of doing things" must be taught. A few small businesses pay attention to the importance of this process. Having a documented "organizational culture" or "the way we do it here" program is essential for any organization. Here are some good reasons:

- It helps new employees learn how people in the company think and helps them transition into the team.
- It helps new employees understand the spirit of the company founder.
- It gives employees guidelines to operate within the "we feeling."
- It helps management hire or fire people who fit or don't fit the program.
- It gives customers and vendors an impression of the company that is also reflected in each employee.

To establish these types of programs, management should take the lead and make a continuous, disciplined effort to keep the program in front of the employees on a frequent basis.

There are different ways to go about building a corporate culture. It is very important that the culture include the organization's values, visions, norms, working language, systems, symbols, beliefs, and habits.

One can hire management consultants or send the employees to leadership training. However, it all starts with the owner of the company. The owner-operator is most often a successful entrepreneur who understands customer needs and the value of excellent service. For a company to grow and be successful, these attributes should be taught to all employees regardless of their function. That is a big challenge: How do you train the salespeople, the accounting staff, and the drivers so that they interpret and use the corporate culture in a unified way? A program for organizational culture should include:

- **Mission:** strategic direction and intent; goals, objectives, and vision
- **Adaptability:** creating change, customer focus, and organizational learning
- **Involvement:** empowerment, team orientation, and capability development
- **Consistency:** core values, agreement, coordination, and integration

If you are the owner-operator and want to implement a program of this kind, you must take charge and drive the topic within your organization. The first step is to assemble other leaders within your company and get them to go along with the idea. Once you have a core group, you can decide how to build a program and how to implement it. You can choose the "do it yourself" method, which is as easy as writing down a few guidelines and presenting them to your employees, or you can choose a more advanced method by selecting one of many management programs and adapting it to your business. A more sophisticated approach is to hire an outside coach who works with you and your employees on a regular basis. Regardless of what approach you take, it is very important to keep your program in front of the members of the organization.

If your corporate culture program gets traction, you have to balance what you do. You can't drive it so hard that employees perceive it as a cult or an exercise in brainwashing. Some employees welcome these types of structures and some don't. The ones that don't can be divided into two categories: those that will adapt and those that won't. If you have employees that don't want to participate in your corporate culture program, they are better off somewhere else. That needs to be brought to their attention sooner rather than later. When an employee chooses to not blend in with the company culture and resists change, termination may be the only choice.

The benefits of implementing and maintaining a strong organizational culture is that you, the owner, will see more clearly the areas of your business that need improvement. The employees will be more engaged and comfortable with their positions and therefore able to give you recommendations for improvements that may not have been pointed out to you otherwise. Customers, vendors and other stakeholders to your business will see the company as one organization that represents certain values. All employees, regardless of position, are aligned with that value and strive for the same goal.

Building an organizational culture takes a lot of time, effort, and determination, but it is an investment that will make your business better.

CHAPTER 7

Security and Safety

COMPARED TO THE RETAIL INDUSTRY, dealing with security in the portable storage industry is a cake walk. What percent of the population is dead-set on stealing a storage unit? Additionally, our rental contracts protect us from issues surrounding what might happen to the contents of our containers at a customer's site. But our relatively good position in the security world is far from comfortable. We still have plenty to consider on this important topic.

Securing Your Rental Boxes

PHIL HERNDON

Breaking into a container is not easy, but not totally preventable. It can be done if the thieves have enough time, privacy, and tools. Some years back we discovered that a semi-tractor had wrapped chains around the door locking bars and pulled the container around the yard until the doors came apart. Despite the rarity of theft, it is our responsibility to do all we can to provide a reasonably secure site and storage box.

The Lock Box

The lock box is the industry standard for security and has been a formidable opponent to many would-be thieves. The lock box is simply a small section of steel tubing cut in a 6-inch section, plated on top, and welded either to the right door or to the interior right door locking rod. The lock box, in the closed position, fits over a pad eye that has been welded (or bolted) to the container door. This low-cost box provides protection against pad lock tampering. Many of the container component suppliers offer ready to install lock boxes.

Potential violations of the lock box include spraying the lock with Freon until it crystallizes, sawing off the pad eye between the box and the container door and pulling on the lock box with a chain until it fails. Again, this type of tampering takes time and tools.

For added security we have begun to add angle iron to the stationary side of the door to protect against someone sawing the pad eye from the side or top. This helps protect the pad eye from a reciprocating saw. In addition, we have upgraded the pad eye to ¼-inch bar stock. I am sure that many of you have come up with similar design enhancements to increase the effectiveness of the lock box.

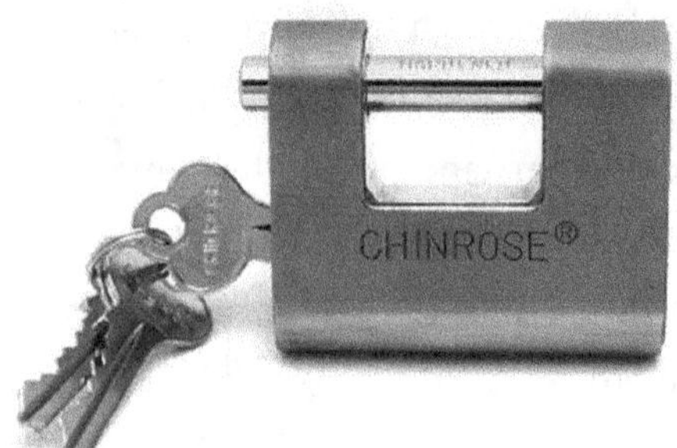

Source: CHINROSE International

Many of the new-build containers come with a lock box already installed. Because the lock box has to fit within the ISO dimensions of the container, the space for the lock is limited. For these lock boxes a block lock works well and is very secure, although they do cost more than a typical 2-inch pad lock. As an alternative for single-trip boxes that are added into our rental fleet we modify the lock box so it can accommodate a regular pad lock.

Hybrid and Proprietary Systems

An internal locking system is another option that is commonly used for custom-built storage containers or modified fleets. Some have a proprietary design, but the concept centers on increased security with ease of operation by keeping as much of the locking mechanism inside the container, away from torches and saws. We have discussed designing our own system, but we have yet to begin any work.

Another solution is a heavy lock that wraps completely around the lock rod handle and latch. This heavy block of plated steel is tamper resistant and provides a reasonable shield. The lock is integral to the unit. Keys have to be provided to each customer.

Steel straps that wrap around and secure to the lock rods are useable on most ISO-style storage units. This design holds the doors closed by connecting the two inner lock rods on each door. I have never seen one of these in field use, but they look secure.

Most recently I have seen an internal lock that is opened with a transmitter that sends an encrypted code. The code releases the lock when the transmitter touches the steel door. It's a cool and sophisticated solution for customers who are willing to pay extra for the latest in security technology.

If you are building a rental fleet and considering a security method beyond the typical industry lock box, you need to consider one key issue: managing the keys! Customers will lose them, break them off in the lock, or remove your lock thinking that it is theirs. Portable storage industry customers are usually comfortable with providing their own lock or, in some cases, buying a lock from the rental company. Additionally, recouping the cost of a hybrid locking system seems like an uphill battle. With that said, it's important to not be blind to emerging technology. Don't wake up someday to find out you are the last company to make the shift to a better locking system!

Who Is Responsible for Security at Your Customer's Location?

Every lease agreement needs to include these words: "The rental company is not responsible for any loss or damage associated with the use or rental of this equipment including loss from break in. Additionally, the customer is liable for any damage or loss to the rental equipment while it is in their possession." In my company we are lean on fine print, hoping that fewer words will have a better chance of being read and understood. It is in your best interest to establish very clearly to your customers that security is their responsibility.

Let's not forget that providing security is the primary reason most customers require portable storage. We as operators need to do all we can to provide the most secure unit for our customers.

Occupational Fraud: When Your Employees Steal from You!

ANDERS NORLIN

I have visited many companies in the portable storage industry, as well as companies in peripheral industries. I often hear stories of fraud, embezzlement, and theft by employees. I also find that not until a company has been defrauded do they start to think of how to implement controls and routines to prevent fraud and theft. The Association of Certified Fraud Examiners recently published a report based on more than 1,800 fraud cases during 2008 and 2009. The methods, issues, and challenges of fraud are no different today.

Here are some highlights of their findings:

- The estimated average loss from fraud is equivalent to 5 percent of a company's revenue.
- Small businesses are disproportionately victimized by occupational fraud.
- Occupational fraud is mostly discovered by an anonymous tip than by the owners or auditors.
- The median time between the start of a fraudulent activity and discovery is eighteen months.
- Anti-fraud controls are rarely implemented in small businesses.
- Most fraud occurs in accounting, operations, and sales departments.
- Fraud perpetrators send out warning signals while engaging in illicit activities.
- About 85 percent of fraud perpetrators are first-time offenders.

Occupational fraud is defined as: the use of one's occupation for personal enrichment through the deliberate misuse or misapplication of the employing organization's resources or assets. This is a very broad definition. The schemes range from petty thefts, such as an employee pilfering from the company's supplies, to very complex financial statement fraud. However, what is most important for an employer is that all fraud involves a violation of trust. It doesn't matter if the fraud is a simple manipulation of a time sheet or outright theft of assets or money. The perpetrator has shown that he or she is no longer trustworthy.

Occupational fraud is divided into three categories:

- *Corruption:* bribery, illegal gratuities, purchasing, and sales schemes, as well as economic extortion.
- *Fraudulent Statements:* illegal time sheets, fraudulent resumes, or overstating equipment values.
- *Asset Misappropriation (most common):* skimming cash and deliveries, larceny, billing schemes, check tampering, false expense reimbursements, fake payroll claims, fudged inventories, and unauthorized tool use.

Although asset misappropriation is the most common type of occupational fraud, it is the least costly per incident. It is difficult for employers to monitor numerous small incidents, which makes fraud more likely to occur undetected. Most incidents involve the accounting department. The second most common fraud involves trusted employees who have constant access to the employer's assets.

The stereotype of an individual who commits occupational fraud in the accounting department is a person who has worked with the firm for a very long time, knows a lot about the owner's personal economy, and hardly ever takes a long leave from his or her work. The report found that 67 percent of accounting fraud is committed by men and 33 percent by women. Both genders range in age between thirty and fifty years at the time the fraud is discovered. The losses take about eighteen months to discover and they are, when discovered, in the range of $250,000 per incident for men and $100,000 for women. The amount of the loss is also related to the tenure of the employee, which makes sense. If I am committing undetected fraud over a long tenure, then my fraudulent monetary gain will increase. Furthermore, perpetrators tend to increase the amounts by which they defraud their employers the longer they go undetected.

How to Prevent Occupational Fraud

- Set up a hotline that allows employees to anonymously report fraud and complaints to management. This allows employees to communicate without the fear of repercussions from an immediate superior who may be the perpetrator.
- Train your employees to look for fraud. It gives the organization a better understanding of the issue and gives a potential perpetrator a reason to have second thoughts about crossing the line.
- Look for odd behavior, such as employees that have strange reasons for why things are missing (i.e. books not balancing or related reports being late or out of date).
- Learn about your employees' personal situations. When you see an employee with a standard of living that's higher than expected, given his or her salary, it is worthwhile to find out how that is possible.
- Organize surprise audits using someone other than your regular CPA. To avoid making potential perpetrators suspicious, present the audit as an insurance or banking audit.
- Create job rotation programs so there is no position that is understood by only one employee.
- Establish routines for opening and date stamping inbound mail.

- Establish policies and routines for signing checks, authorizing outgoing payments, and ordering supplies that involve several individuals; also rotate their positions.
- Have payments sent to a bank lock box or the company's CPA firm.
- Establish frequent and random drug testing for all employees.

It is obvious that occupational fraud is a dilemma for all businesses. Therefore, implement controls and routines for the purpose of preventing fraud. Don't be afraid to talk about your concerns with your employees. It may lead to a potential perpetrator not crossing the line. Furthermore, don't be afraid to talk to business colleagues about situations in which you have been defrauded. It may help you resolve the problem, or you may help someone else avoid ending up in your situation.

Protecting Your Business

PHIL HERNDON

It's a weird feeling when you came home from an evening out and find that someone has been inside your house, trashed the place, and taken your valuables. You quickly realize that anger is about more than the missing items; it's the personal violation. Someone came into your house, the place you hold as safe and private, and violated your life. It's normal to feel shaken up. Likewise, business owners feel violated when someone steals from us. It's personal!

A few years ago, at an NPSA annual conference, Tom Long of Long Vans in Wisconsin asked if we could take a few minutes during the operators' roundtable discussion to share our experiences with theft and fraud. Tom had a story about a friend who was robbed by an employee (see the first case below). We opened the discussion to about two hundred people in attendance. The room went quiet. As the moderator, I filled the silence with two examples (see the second and third cases below). No one shared anything, so we moved to another discussion topic.

An hour later we closed the session. As the room emptied out, to my surprise, five people came to me with their stories of how they had been robbed (cases four through nine below). They were not willing to share their stories publicly! So, while retaining their anonymity, I will share here some thought provoking ways you can be robbed.

Case Studies

Case 1: Double Entry Accounting

The employee input the same bill twice with a slight variation in the invoice number so that it would appear to be an excusable error. Then, when it came time to print checks, she changed the vendor name to a company that happened to be owned by her husband. After the checks were printed, she changed the name back to the company that was a regular vendor.

Prevention method: QuickBooks has an activity log report that's got enough detail to show this type of maneuver. Since fewer and fewer banks provide canceled checks, observing the activity log is your best bet. However, it requires a good understanding of who your customers and vendors are.

Case 2: Inventory Control

As purchased containers entered the yard, the yard manager did not record them. Then he sold them for cash.

Prevention method: This type of stealing requires several employees to know what is going on. Additionally, most of us are small enough to know what is coming in and going out just by looking out the window. By walking the yard on a regular basis, you can observe the changes, the comings and goings. This is typically an effective form of prevention. Also, an equipment interchange report (EIR) is a document system used by depots to account for all in-and-out gate activity. When the equipment enters the yard, the driver checks-in at the office and receives an EIR. When the container is unloaded, the lift operator takes the EIR from the driver and notes any changes. Then the EIR goes to the yard office for system input.

Case 3: Accounts Payable

In the process of converting to new accounting software and training employees, this manager set himself up as a vendor on auto pay! The amount was small enough that no one questioned it on the monthly bank statement, until the total exceeded $200,000. Finally, someone asked, "Who is this vendor?"

Prevention method: If you're small, take the time to know your vendors. If you are too big to do that, assign two employees on a rotational basis to periodically validate vendors and customers.

Case 4: Answer the Phone

A salesperson was positive and energetic but seemed to have spotty results. He was regularly left in the office unsupervised to cover incoming customer calls. The owner, on a hunch, installed a phone recording device. A week later, the recorder revealed that the salesperson was referring customers to a competitor who was compensating the employee on the side.

Prevention method: Our phones have a call history function, and we look at it regularly. We take note of who called and chat about what they wanted. But unless you record all conversations, I am not sure how to catch this type of fraud, and I'm not even sure if it's legal to record phone calls.

Case 5: The Cash Drawer

This type of fraud is simple and common. The customer offers a cash payment and the salesperson or payables receiving clerk reduces the sale amount in the books (if it's even recorded) and pockets the difference.

Prevention method: An open office with a full recording of all cash transactions is usually good protection. Every well-run business with cash transactions has multiple and constantly changing methods of watching cash transactions.

Case 6: Scrap Metal

Jeff was a good shop foreman who always came in early, had everything set up, and kept the shop busy. Every day he parked his truck next to the shop's side door. One day the local scrap metal company called to ask if we were aware that almost daily Jeff was bringing in a pickup load of scrap metal and aluminum!

Prevention method: Be sure to get out of the office and look around. It would have been easy enough to see the scrap metal in this guy's pickup at the end of every shift if the owner had walked past his truck!

Case 7: No Time Off?

The receivable clerk had not taken a vacation in years. Finally, the business owner compelled the employee to take two weeks off.

During that time, the bank called and asked how the cash was to be processed. The bank staff didn't know because no cash had been deposited for years!

Prevention method: Shift responsibilities around occasionally. You can call it cross-training, but make sure that no one is an island.

Case 8: Office Supplies

We all know that print cartridges are expensive. This employee took care of buying all the office supplies and in the process was able to keep her family supplied and even personally sell "surplus" supplies.

Prevention method: As with case 7 above, the best prevention method is to shift responsibilities, ask questions, and look at receipts and inventory.

Case 9: Multiple Books

A single-user version of QuickBooks was the perfect opportunity for this employee to create a near identical company in her computer. The phantom company was used for all cash transactions. She produced customer invoices and a screen on her computer that looked legitimate. By the time she was found out, thousands of dollars were stolen.

Prevention method: Have a multiple-user version of QuickBooks, or use QuickBooks Online. Many of us also have separate inventory tracking systems that allow for a faceoff with accounting transactions.

Your Defensive Plan

There is no end to the possibilities for stealing, but there are several reoccurring tactics used by perpetrators. Addressing the known methods of preventing theft can help tremendously in protecting your business. They include:

Maintain an open work environment: If your employees are isolated, they will find it easier to develop systems that can't be easily detected. When you walk into a work area, be aware of how your employees respond. Closing a computer screen or suddenly rearranging a desk can be signs that your employee is up to something he or she doesn't want you to see. Also, after-hours is always a good time to look for "paper clips" in your employees' desks! The next day, tell them you took some paper clips out of their desk drawers so that they are reminded of the non-private nature of the office, desk, files, and computers.

Shift tasks and responsibilities: If you require staff to be cross-trained and to cover for each other, you have eliminated an opportunity for an employee to hide theft during the work flow. In our office, each of us creates invoices, inputs payables, and receives payments. As a result, accounting is everyone's concern, not just a single person's. Frankly, I like this approach better because it's more efficient to enter a bill into the system than it is to approve the bill and then pass it to someone else for input.

Don't be lazy: When an owner stops looking at physical inventory, starts trusting a computer screen to be accurate, and stops monitoring employee activity, the door is open for a thief. We don't have log books, inventory cards, or cancelled checks, so the traditional paper trail is no more. As owners, we should take the time to ask about an unfamiliar vendor, about cost increases for materials, or about where a box was delivered.

Be an example: When *you* pocket incoming cash, or when you have employees do personal work for you, or when you unload only half of the supplies you bought for the office and take the rest home, then you are setting a bad example. In a small business, it's hard to keep clear lines between business and personal. Should I charge myself for the storage of my car inside a 20-foot container in our yard? Probably not. But I do know which credit card to use for personal purchases. I am not attempting to turn your moral compass. I simply want to point out that you should set a moral standard for your employees.

We each run our businesses our own way. Some of us allow our employees to take a little out of the till every so often and consider that part of their benefits. Others control things so tightly that we would notice a misused postage stamp! It's your business. Do as you choose but be consistent and comfortable in that. Sadly, stealing is woven into the fabric of our society. As Mark Twain wrote in his essay *Advice for Good Little Boys,* "You ought never to take anything that don't belong to you—if you cannot carry it off."

The Discipline of Operating Safely

As a small operator, I don't have the luxury (or burden) of employing a staff safety or risk manager who helps us with safety and risk issues. It falls on the owner to think about those things that might cause damage or loss to the company and its employees. From identity theft to container theft, from employee physical injury to loss of market share, we have plenty to worry about. I share here my top-three risks and what I try to do to mitigate their impact.

Worker Safety

I would sooner lose my entire business than allow one of my employees to be seriously injured or die in the line of work. This goes beyond money (pay or insurance coverage) because when an employer loses an employee to a permanently disabling injury or death, much more than the company is impacted. I don't want to bad-mouth safety meetings, but we should not depend on them to create a culture of safety. That starts with the owner. If the owner is not willing to purchase safe tools or stop work when an unsafe condition is observed, then the employees will not see the importance of keeping a safe workplace. I have fired employees for disregarding basic safety practices. I once had to fire an employee who didn't comply with three warnings that he should not leave a sledgehammer on the safety cage above the forklift seat (true story).

Injuries are rarely caused by freak accidents. When a container is properly lifted, or when a tilt trailer is fully functional, or when a truck has been regularly serviced and inspected, the physical causes of accidents are reduced. The rest is up to us humans to be careful. I had a worker injure his arm while stepping out of the office. He was so taken by our young female bookkeeper that he jumped over the stair railing and landed on his elbow. Stupid. But that was our only claim for six years!

Working with longshoremen in the port, before I started my company, there seemed to be no end to accidents caused by human error. Thankfully, no one on my watch was seriously hurt. But all my experience shows that accidents happen when people don't follow simple safety rules. Keep your team focused on safety and show them how important they are to you by valuing workplace safety.

A few years back, I flew in a small private plane with a friend (he built it!). As we were preparing to leave, he handed me a long list of questions and had me read each one to him. In response, he showed me that each part of the plane was checked and operating correctly. It took a full ten minutes. During our trip, we took off and landed three times. At each departure, he had me read the questions, proving that we were safe to fly. Safety and risk reduction is directly related to the discipline of practicing safety.

Recently, a 20-foot container decided to follow another container being lifted out of a stack. Fortunately, the lift driver saw what was happening. We were able to get the rogue container safely to the ground. With hydraulic equipment controls and limited visibility, it's no surprise when things like that happen. So, I encourage my employees to be "aware operators." Thankfully, in eighteen years, we have had only four lost days due to injuries and no serious injuries. What follows is my agenda for monthly safety meetings. We do our best to hold a meeting the first of each month!

January: Working in cold conditions.

Objective: Remind staff of limits in cold conditions.

Although I work in a temperate climate, the winter cold can still impact safe work practices. Coats and hoods limit visibility and mobility. There is less natural light, which reduces working and driving visibility. Be mindful of working limits, allow for reduced mobility, slow down if visibility is reduced, and keep equipment in good working conditions. Don't work in icy conditions, or assume that what you can't see is safe, or let loose clothing get caught in machinery.

February: Watch out for water.

Objective: Raise awareness about water and a safe workplace.

Back when it used to rain in California, this was a big issue. Rain can flood shop floors, increase the size and number of potholes in the yard, and reduce visibility for drivers dealing with traffic challenges. So, be sure that your trucks have good windshield wipers and that drivers slow down when visibility is poor. Also confirm that rain gear is in good shape and that electrical connections and junctions are dry and well-grounded. Avoid working in standing water or risk getting soaked!

March: See others.

Objective: Know where people are.

About ten years ago we were loading a 40-foot box on a chassis with a forklift when the lift driver thought the rear far corner of the container was on the chassis twist lock. It wasn't. When he backed away from the container, it fell off the chassis on to its side. Where was the driver? Thankfully, he was not on the other side!

Many yards require drivers to stay in their trucks. We don't require that, but we do require that they stay in sight. We encourage you to make sure you stay in view and that you acknowledge the presence of others, making your movements intentional and predictable. You should avoid being between moving objects and avoid approaching a truck or lift from behind.

April: Have a plan.

Objective: Know the plan for a disaster or damaging event.

Thanks to a plethora of government agencies, we have developed a disaster plan, a meeting place, clearly marked locations for fire extinguishers, and a segregated location for hazardous materials. We have a protocol for how to handle a fire or material spill. It's important for you to report incidents if they happen, get help when needed, follow the plan you have developed, and protect yourself. Don't try to be a hero. Never cover up an incident, or ignore the plan, or guess what to do.

May: Fix it or report it.

Objective: Stay safe with good working equipment.

We work hard at making sure our shop and rolling stock is in safe working condition. Broken equipment is unsafe and reduces efficiency. You should report damaged or broken equipment, use tools and equipment properly, and take time to repair equipment. You should avoid using broken tools and equipment. Never cut off the ground prong on a power plug or disconnect electrical grounds. And don't use damaged winch cables.

June: Walk through a disaster.
Objective: Reinforce the plan.

We addressed this topic in the guidelines for April, but this time we walk through a mock disaster. We start from the incident location and continue until we are waiting outside for assistance at the designated gathering spot. As always you should report all incidents, get help, and follow the plan while protecting yourself.

July: Stay healthy.
Objective: Remind employees of the need to be healthy workers.

Although we provide sick days off, sometimes employees think they can't miss work no matter how bad they feel. Also, some workers will use bad body mechanics and injure themselves. Use your brain instead of your back, use tools correctly, keep your work area clean, be focused, and get help if you need it. Avoid taking unsafe short cuts, and don't rush a job or work while you are injured.

August: Use space wisely.
Objective: Encourage orderly work spaces.

Because containers are large, you need plenty of space to work on them. Keeping nonessential equipment, tools, parts, and people clear of the work area is important. Also removal of scrap or fabrication debris helps keep the work area safe. Be sure to respect the work area of each shop member, to pick up after yourself, and to stack containers squarely. Avoid leaving a mess, blocking passage ways, or keeping extra air hoses and power cords in your work area.

September: Unnecessary pressure.

Objective: Properly manage pressure on the work schedule.

We go through periods when we have more work than we have mechanics or drivers. The fact is only so much work can happen in a given period, so pressure to increase output can result in injury, damage, or poor quality. That's why it is important to keep shop and truck schedules up-to-date, to resist the pressure to pile on more work, and to manage customer expectations. We recommend not allowing customer pressure to compromise the work schedule, or force people to skip breaks, or cause staff to cut corners while trying to get more work done.

October: Wear your protection.

Objective: Remind workers of the need for protection.

Our work requires good nonskid shoes. When welding, you should use proper protection for skin, eyes, and ears. Our tools have built-in protections: grinders, saws, and nail guns. Because all our power tools are shared, it's everyone's responsibility to make sure they are safe. Ensure that your staff uses tools properly. Remember to fix bent or broken safety guards. However, don't remove the safety guards, don't use broken tools, and don't bypass safety switches.

November: Be qualified.

Objective: Identify skill levels of equipment operation.

Our big trucks require a specific driver's license. However, our yard and shop lifts can be operated by anyone. So we have to self-police our yard operators. The controls of a fork or container lift are simple but operating them can be another story. Knowing the limitations and safe way to operate equipment is important. Make sure that your team has been checked out on each piece of equipment.

Report damage or malfunctioning equipment and stay within safe working loads. Never overload machines or use them incorrectly and avoid lifting items higher than is necessary.

December: Review the year's safety practices.
Objective: Raise attention on safe practices.
Host a company lunch to talk about safety. This list may not be a perfect idea, but after years of talking about doing this, I now have a framework from which to conduct safety meetings. This was long overdue, so now I need to hold the meetings!

Loss of Assets or Equipment

There are other safety and security matters that are related to protecting and insuring your fleet. You don't have to talk to many bankers to be reminded of the "scary side" of our business. When they say, "I think I understand your business, but how does that work? You own these assets, but they are spread over hundreds of locations within a one-hundred-mile radius. How can you keep track of them? What if they are stolen? Do you lose them? No title? Well, how are they secured? What if there is a fire? How are they insured?" If we thought like bankers we would not be in the business we are in. Yes, there are risks.

So how can we reduce the risk of inventory loss? There are at least three things we do. First, standardize your rental fleet. It helps your marketing and it also helps improve security. When your containers' color, markings, and condition are consistent across your fleet, potential thieves will find it harder to move and hide your equipment. In addition, the honest people will call you and let you know that any stolen boxes seem to be in the wrong place.

Second, make sure that you manage your fleet. I have yet to find a rental customer who will send me monthly checks for a container they do not have. When a customer does not pay and cannot be reached, it's a good time to do a physical check of your container. These situations are rare, but I don't like to lose my boxes!

Third, take some time to photograph your fleet. We recently acquired two competitors and in the acquisition process we took a picture of each container on-rent. Last January, when we were throwing a tennis ball against the wall waiting for the phone to ring, it occurred to me to photograph all our boxes on-rent. So, we went out, found each box, and took a picture of it. Thankfully there were no problems, but we plan on making this a regular event, maybe every two years.

These three actions have helped me settle my concerns about lost inventory, but I don't plan on forgetting about this risk anytime soon.

General Liability

Someone called recently to claim that we cracked his windshield. Another person claimed that we broke a concrete entry while delivering a rental box. It helps to know what you are and are not responsible for. There is no substitute for an insurance agent who is responsive and knows your business. If you don't know yours, look at making a change! Don't sidestep responsibility, but also don't roll over!

These are petty things, but what about the big exposures? Thankfully, containers are a harmless product. Storage boxes are hard to burn, they don't pollute, and on the ground, they can't cause bodily injury. Having a good rental contract, making sure that your driver's have release forms, investing in a clean and newer rental fleet, and building a professional staff are all simple things that can reduce your exposure and help you sleep at night.

Cybersecurity: Another Safety Concern for Your Business

ANDERS NORLIN

Broadband, Internet, email, text messaging, and other information technologies are powerful tools for small businesses reaching new markets and for increasing productivity and efficiency. However, companies should have a cybersecurity strategy to protect the business, the customers, and the data from growing cybersecurity threats. Cyber crooks are out there all the time, so keep updating and improving your safety tools and routines. Here are some suggestions for how you can protect yourself from the demons of the Internet.

Train employees in security principles. Designate the task of cyber-security to a few trusted employees and make sure they are cross-trained in the case of absence or termination of employment. Establish basic security practices and policies for employees, such as requiring strong passwords and regular password updates. Establish appropriate Internet use guidelines that detail penalties for violating company cybersecurity policies. Establish rules of behavior that describe how to handle and protect customer information and other vital data.

Protect information from cyber-attacks. Installing the latest security software, web browser, and operating system are the best defenses against viruses, malware, and other online threats. Set antivirus software to run a scan after each update. Install other key software updates as soon as they are available.

Provide firewall security for your Internet connection. A fire-wall is a set of related programs that prevent outsiders from accessing data on a private network. Make sure the operating system's firewall is enabled or install free firewall software available online. If employees work from home, ensure that their home system(s) are protected by a firewall.

Create a mobile device action plan. Mobile devices can create significant security and management challenges, especially if they hold confidential information or can access the corporate network. Require users to password protect their devices, encrypt their data, and install security apps to prevent criminals from stealing information while the phone is on public networks. Be sure to set reporting procedures for lost or stolen equipment.

Make backup copies of important business information. Regularly backup the data on all computers. Critical data includes word processing documents, electronic spreadsheets, databases, financial files, human resources files, and accounts receivable/payable files. Backup data automatically, if possible, or at least weekly, and store the copies either offsite or in the cloud.

Control physical access to your computers. Prevent unauthorized individuals from using business computers. Laptops can be easy targets for theft, or they can be lost, so lock them up when unattended. Make sure a separate user account is created for each employee and require strong passwords. Administrative privileges should only be given to trusted IT staff and key personnel.

Secure your wireless networks. If you have a wireless network for your workplace, make sure it is secure, encrypted and hidden. To hide your network, set up your wireless access point or router so it does not broadcast the network name, known as the Service Set Identifier (SSID). Password protect access to the router.

Employ best practices on payment cards. Work with banks or payment processors to ensure that trusted tools and anti-fraud services are being used. You may also have additional security obligations pursuant to agreements with your bank or processor. Isolate payment systems from other, less secure programs, and don't use the same computer to process payments and surf the Internet.

Limit employee access to data and information. Do not provide any employee with access to all data systems. Employees should only be given access to the specific data systems that they need for their jobs. They should not be able to install any software without permission. Do not allow visitors to download information on your computers from USB sticks or other portable devices.

Use best practices for passwords and authentication. Require employees to use unique passwords and to change passwords every three months. Consider implementing multi-factor authentication that requires additional information beyond a password to gain entry. Check with your vendors that handle sensitive data, especially financial institutions, to see if they offer multi-factor authentication for your account.

More Electronic Information Leads to More Tax Identity Theft

Don't stick your head in the sand. The risk of tax identity theft, whether of Social Security Numbers or Employer Identification Numbers, is real. The US Federal Trade Commission (FTC) recently reported that there were almost five hundred thousand complaints of identity theft in 2015. Over half of those complaints were tax identity thefts. As individuals, we have become aware of identity theft and the need to protect our personal, online information.

This includes credit card numbers, Social Security Numbers, medical records, and other information.

Businesses also need to be aware of the risk of tax identity theft they face. Most of the attention has been paid to individual victims of tax identity theft, which is a scam that occurs when a stolen SSN is used to file a tax return and claim a fraudulent tax refund. The victim is often unaware that his SSN has been used for a fraudulent return until he files his own tax return and learns that one has already been filed. The US Government Accountability Office found that the IRS paid out $5.8 billion in fraudulent refunds for the 2013 tax year.

Another SSN scam occurs when a fraudster uses a stolen SSN to obtain a job. The employer reports that person's income to the IRS under the stolen SSN. Unaware of the income that has been reported against the stolen SSN, the victim will not include those earnings when filing his or her tax return. The IRS records will indicate that the victim has underreported income.

How are SSN's stolen? The thefts can often be traced to the victim's place of employment. Insiders at a company may steal the numbers as well as employee or customer information. Perpetrators also might wait until staff members let their guards down and leave SSNs readily accessible on computers or in the trash. Individuals may also be careless with their SSNs and personal information. While large companies are favorite targets, the improper use of just a single SSN can wreak havoc for one of your employees or customers. So, smaller companies are also at risk. Tax identity theft is a top concern for the IRS.

The IRS will be implementing new requirements and is working with the payroll industry to put new safeguards in place. The Protecting Americans from Tax Hikes (PATH) Act, signed in late

2015, requires employers to file W-2, W-3, and 1099 forms by January 31 of the year following the tax year. That way, it is easier for the IRS to catch discrepancies between legitimate forms filed by employers and those filed by fraudsters seeking refunds based on false forms before the agency sends out refund checks. The earlier deadline takes effect for statements filed in 2017 for the 2016 tax year.

The IRS is also expected to expand a pilot program to verify the authenticity of W-2 data submitted by taxpayers on electronically filed tax returns. For the pilot program, the IRS partnered with major payroll services to provide a sixteen-digit code and a new verification code field on a limited number of W-2 copies for employees. Each unique number is derived from data on the form itself and is known only to the IRS, the payroll service provider, and the employee.

In addition to stolen SSNs, cyber thieves are also going after EINs. This is a challenge for the many businesses that put more effort into protecting SSNs than their EINs. A fraudster could use a stolen EIN to report false income and or withholding and file for a refund. In addition to the fraudulent refund from the use of a stolen EIN, an EIN in the wrong hands could result in incorrectly reported payroll tax withholdings leading the IRS to scrutinize the employer. As with SSN theft victims, EIN theft victims may not discover something is amiss until they file their tax returns and receive IRS notification that they had already filed for that tax year.

Here are some tips for preventing tax identity theft:

- Use antivirus and other security software on all workplace computers.
- Update your data security plans regularly in response to new risks.

- Educate employees about phishing schemes.
- Keep SSNs, EINs, and other sensitive information in a secure location and restrict access on a need-to-know basis.
- Update business filings with the IRS and your government's secretary of state when contact information changes.
- Monitor credit reports, IRS and state tax authority accounts, and other business filings.
- File tax returns and W-2s, W-3s, and 1099s as early as possible.
- Develop an action strategy for dealing with tax identity theft, including identifying who to notify in the event of theft.

Remember that the IRS does not initiate contact with taxpayers by email, text messages, or social media to request personal or financial information.

Risk, Chance, and Uncertainty

ANDERS NORLIN

We all know that life is uncertain. The unknown can upend what we think should or could happen. Daily life for businesses and individuals is exposed to uncertainty and risk. Uncertainty comes from a range of possible positive and negative things (excellent, good, acceptable, bad, or terrible) that might happen. Although we can't overcome uncertainty, we can prepare ourselves for those outcomes.

Risk Taking Based on Statistics

High-level business statistics are often used to understand the exposure to various outcomes in life. For example, the life insurance industry has large amounts of data that measure the risks of insuring people of different ages, locations, professions, etc. The life insurance company takes an educated risk, based on the historic information presented in the statistical data.

Risk Taking Based on Knowledge

In most daily situations, we do not have statistical data available when we need to decide with an element of risk. In those situations, we make decisions based on our knowledge. Knowledge and awareness of risk can vary widely depending on age, education, experience, personal upbringing, and life in general.

Risk Awareness

The same event can be perceived as having different levels of risk, depending on each decision-maker's situation. There is personal risk, in which individuals have a higher risk tolerance for themselves than for a group. There is risk of others, which is related to an individual's perception of the risk compared to the perception of others. And there is the influence of age on risk perception. Awareness increases with age, experience, and education. The lowest risk awareness is found in teen boys age thirteen to sixteen.

Luck

Sometimes an unforeseen change has a positive impact and sometimes it has negative impact. When a positive change suddenly appears, we call it good luck. When something negative suddenly appears, we call it bad luck. But what is luck for a business?

Luck is: an event that occurs independently of the key actions of the company; an event that has significant consequences (negative or positive) for the company; or an event that has some element of unpredictability.

Luck happens. The key is what to do with it. Jim Collins, the author of *Great by Choice,* describes four outcomes on luck, depending on how the situation is managed.

Great Return on Bad Luck	Great Return on Good Luck
Poor Return on Bad Luck	Poor Return on Good Luck

Here are some examples of outcomes, depending on how luck is managed.

Great Return on Luck

- Turning a bad luck situation into an opportunity, by handling those affected so that they feel well cared for despite the negative outcome. This improves the company's image.
- Turning a good luck situation into a great result for your company, thanks to the positive situation that was created.

Poor Return on Luck

- Making a bad luck situation worse, by avoiding the situation and not trying to minimize the damage.
- Not reacting to the opportunity created by a good luck situation and missing the chance of improving one way or the other.

As you can see, the poor return on luck, good or bad, is an effect of being passive rather than acting. You cannot plan for luck, but you can be prepared to manage luck by:

Building flexibility into your organization so that you can quickly react to a good or bad luck situation. In our industry, that can mean having extra tools, a backup driver or back up truck, as well as a good relationship with a competitor in case you run out of containers to rent.

Developing knowledge so that your business is not disrupted by a good or bad luck situation. For example, learn about the local traffic patterns so you are prepared for congestion, accidents, and mechanical breakdowns on the road. Have access to enough containers so that you can respond to urgent customer needs.

Prepare your business for handling a situation of bad luck. Some examples are:

- A key employee suddenly leaving
- Your trucks breaking down
- Theft of critical machines and tools
- Extended power outages, floods, or other natural disasters

The more educated we are about what can happen, the better we can manage the unforeseen events and what they bring. These are challenges and/or opportunities. However, education comes with a cost, and it may be a waste if nothing unforeseen happens. The future is always bright, so manage your company by being aware that unknowns are going to bring more good than bad.

CHAPTER 8

Finance

IT IS NO SURPRISE that Anders shines in this chapter. I learned everything I know about finance for portable storage business from Anders. So, Anders deserves credit for even the parts of this chapter that I wrote. As with other business disciplines addressed in this book, your lack of attention to this area could spell the end of your business.

Portable Self Storage Containers: Financing Challenges

ANDERS NORLIN

Financing containers in the portable self-storage industry, or "residential storage industry," is much more challenging than financing in the traditional portable storage industry. The traditional industry uses ISO containers, and a standardized product that is part of a well-established second-hand market. The portable *self-storage* industry uses specialized containers often tied-up in franchising agreements with no established and a restricted second-hand market. Therefore, if you are looking to launch a portable self-storage program, think strategically of what type of containers you choose.

Being a portable storage operator, you have most likely experienced the skepticism with which a banker looks at our industry. Bankers often feel uncomfortable with lending to a portable storage operator because it is complicated to handle a borrower's default. In other words, how does a banker recover and dispose of a container that is used as collateral?

Here are some of the main reasons for a banker's skepticism towards ISO containers:

- The containers are not titled equipment and markings can easily be changed.
- The containers are scattered over a large geographic area.
- Individually, the containers represent a relatively small amount of money.
- The customers of a portable storage company have one or just a few containers per location.

You can overcome these challenges by explaining to the banker that you have your own marking system and that on-hire containers have a rental agreement. Hence, even if the container cannot be recovered, the renter is obligated to pay for the value of the container. Furthermore, if the banker ends up holding a fleet of portable storage containers, it can easily be disposed of. In addition, there are other operators who are willing to buy the on-rent containers and assume the rental agreements. Secondly, there is a sophisticated market for ISO storage containers in most parts of North America. Finally, the physical lifetime for ISO containers is very long.

The banker's view of a fleet of portable self-storage containers would differ in the following areas:

- A larger portion of the containers are at the operator's warehouse.
- The containers are not standardized.
- The secondhand market is not well-developed.

- If the containers are part of a franchise such as PODS, 1-800-PackRat, Units, etc., they may only be sold to other franchisees within the same program.
- The non-standardized container limits a banker's possibilities to sell a fleet that has been repossessed.
- The physical lifespan of portable self-storage containers is shorter than that of an ISO container.

If you are thinking of starting a portable self-storage business or expanding your current operation into one, you need to be strategic about what equipment you choose. From a practical point of view, you want to be able to use the same type of delivery trucks and trailers and from a financial point of view, you should use the products that can most easily be financed. While you may not be looking for financing initially, you may want to do so later; so, you should choose your container equipment with that in mind. Our industry is capital intensive. If your business takes off, you are going to need more capital to grow. That capital can come from investors, lenders, or leasing companies.

Regardless of which you choose, these sources will be exposed to risks involved with the various container types you choose to work with. There are three categories of equipment that financing sources look at.

ISO Containers: These containers are residual equipment from the maritime cargo container industry, also called "one trippers." They are highly standardized products with a long physical lifetime and have a well-established secondhand market.

Portable Self-Storage Containers: These containers have a light construction and are sold directly by a manufacturer or distributor. They have a shorter physical lifespan than the ISO container and they have a limited secondhand market.

Franchisor-Supplied Portable Self-Storage Containers: These are the same as those listed above, but they also have limited resale possibility because they are part of a franchising agreement.

My recommendation, for financing purposes, is that you avoid entering into a franchising agreement so that you can build your fleet with either ISO containers or portable self-storage containers based on which type works best in your market and within your organization.

Financing Options for Your Business

ANDERS NORLIN

Financing is the term for one source of money used in our businesses. Financing typically comes from different sources. There are funds owners contribute to (equity), funds borrowed from banks (loans), funds for specific equipment (leasing), and vendors credit terms (accounts payable). Certain types of financing are suitable for certain parts and stages of our businesses. In the portable storage business, financing is primarily needed for containers and trailers (the equipment that generates income). Secondly, the company needs financing for equipment such as trucks, forklifts, tools, office equipment. Financing is also needed for working capital to pay for the day-to-day operations. Therefore, it is crucial to decide which area you want to finance before you start applying for financing.

Bank loans are the most traditional way of financing a business. Most banks will lend money based on the equity in the company. The loans are relative to the size of the company's equity as well as the company's credibility and that of its principals. The credit rating of the company will, to a large extent, determine the rates and fees charged for the bank's services. Banks supply two different products. They offer credit lines for short-term funds and term loans for equipment with a longer economic lifetime. Typically, the credit line must be paid off at least once every year. Therefore, the credit line is most suitable for financing the trading inventory and operations during periods with low cash balances.

The term loan is suitable for a long-term asset such as containers and trailers. The conditions of the term loan are often related to the value of the equipment. They often require an amortization based on an expected economic lifetime. The loan-to-value is most often in the range of 60 percent to 80 percent of the purchase price of the equipment; the balance has to come from the company's equity. The repayment period often reflects the bank's view of the decline in equipment value, which is rarely representative of the change in market value.

Equipment leasing is a form of financing by which the financial institution takes ownership of the asset and then lets the lessee use it for a monthly or quarterly fee, with an option to purchase the asset in the future. Equipment leases are divided into two principal categories. The first, a finance lease, has a predetermined periodic payment and a purchase option that is less than or equal to 10 percent of the equipment value. The second, an operating lease, has a periodic payment with more flexible terms as far as the number of payments and purchase options. In laymen's terms, the finance lease could be described as an installment purchase, and the operating lease as a rental with an option to purchase.

When to Use Various Types of Financing

Loan financing allows the most flexibility because the funds can be used for most business expenses and equipment within the covenants stipulated by the lender. The cost of a bank loan is by far the least inexpensive way of financing. However, the opportunity cost of the equity used to match the bank loan is often ignored when comparing the cost of loans versus lease financing.

Lease financing is most suitable for revenue generating equipment. The challenge for a lessee is to match the lease expenses with the cash flow generated from the equipment. Typically, lease financing is suitable for capital intensive or rapidly growing companies. The higher cost of the lease financing compared to loan financing can be justified by the ability to finance 100 percent of the equipment cost.

Strategy

Depending on the purpose of the financing and the strategy of the company, different forms of financing are preferable. Typically, companies in our industry finance container-trailers, other equipment, and working capital. All three items are important for the success of the business, but it's the container-trailers that expand the business and increase the revenue. If growth and cash flow is the priority, leasing is clearly the preferred form of financing, followed by loan financing and equity.

Money In and Money Out

PHIL HERNDON

In these times, many of us have found an increased need to be more attentive to accounts payable and accounts receivable. With limited staff, most of us must deal with these tasks ourselves. We have learned that an owner's involvement can have significant impact in these areas. So, maybe it's worth a few words in the SSG?

Accounts Receivable

About five years ago, we began to shift rental billing to rolling four-week cycles. When a customer rents a box, they fall into that week's billing cycle. This eliminates the need for a prorated first invoice and converts a large monthly invoicing task into a manageable weekly task. The final benefit is that is smooths out cash flow. We use QuickBooks Online, which has an easy-to-use, secure credit card function that makes monthly credit card billing about as convenient as possible. While we encourage all rental customers to pay by credit card, only about 5-to-10 percent do. So, let's look at the 90 percent that send us a check every twenty-eight days.

In a normal economy, we find that the first payment sets the tone for a customer's ability to pay on time. However, in the last year we have learned that we need to monitor our accounts receivables closely, watch for pattern changes, and regularly communicate with customers. Some of the factors we have experienced are discussed below.

Time: Contrary to Mick Jagger's voice on my iPod, time is not on my side. Every day that a rental customer does not pay for a box that is on-rent is time without income. It's hard to talk with someone who has no money when you know that they will owe you more for every day that passes! In the old economy, we told customers that we would not pick up the box until they had paid the entire rental amount. In today's world, we discuss options.

Flexibility: We all have to share the load, so businesses regularly offer concessions. We recently had a customer who may have paid us something if we had negotiated earlier. But the customer went completely out of business and we were left with an extended period of no revenue from that client. Our container came back with two pallets of paint and boxes of sprinkler fittings. Currently, we have several customers who have agreed to clear past accounts and pay the rental regularly, but at a discount. We found this solution to be better for both of us.

Communicate: Recently, an occasional customer sent out a form letter that asked for a 10 percent reduction from all of their vendors. In this case, the company is also a supplier to us. We asked our contact in the company if the 10 percent reduction would be reciprocal. We were told no! While it is comical to send something like this, it is also realistic to consider how to share the pain in difficult economic times. That starts with communication, and good communication always starts with understanding. Don't just blast out a compromise offer. Take the time to learn about the customer's situation and then decide if there are options to discuss.

Diligence: The key to collections is to not give up. Customers rarely warn us that they will be late or slow in paying. If you monitor your receivables regularly, you will find that periodic friendly reminders are your best avenue to keeping your accounts receivables in the best condition possible.

As a last resort, there are collection companies. The best service is one that you know, because we have none! I tried a contract collection service that assists with lagging payers and ended up owing them money for service I did not receive. Our current solution is a friend who is an attorney. We find a letter from him is effective in getting a delinquent non-communicating customer to respond.

Accounts Payable

When I was in business school, my accounting teacher taught me to establish a payment schedule for each vendor. The teacher's idea worked like this: Each payment cycle, you mail the check a day later than the date of the previous payment. Continue like that each month. When you hit the point where the vendor is threatening you, then you have set the payment terms for that vendor. Although I don't advocate this method, it demonstrates that common payment terms may or may not be the payment terms that can be used for each vendor. There are times when it's difficult to pay all vendors in thirty days. It requires some finesse to preserve relationships and sources of supply.

Recently, we hit a cash flow bump that was not fun! A client who made a large order was slow to pay, so we quickly ran out of cash. We mapped out projected cash flow through the tight period and developed a minimum payment plan. Proactively, we approached four key vendors with the situation and proposed minimum payments with a commitment to bring our accounts current at our first opportunity. Then it got interesting. Two vendors were willing to take the minimum payments, but they were not willing to sell us any more equipment until our account was paid up. They were not willing to be flexible or trust us, even though we had never missed a payment in eleven years. Thankfully, the other two vendors were more understanding. They allowed us to keep doing business on a case-by-case basis. Once the big check arrived, we caught everybody up and went on with business. We also learned who we could work with in a pinch.

When you are in a tight cash situation, be sure you know the causes. I know of three common reasons, which I share here.

- **Not making money:** If the product you sell costs you more than what you sell it for, you will not make money! Most accounting systems provide good tools for analyzing your costs. Using those tools can help you see your financial health. I know I pay a lot of attention to my volume-related (variable) costs and find that I underestimate the impact of overhead and fixed costs.
- **Surge in business:** When business doubles (that would be nice), you will require twice as much working capital (cash) as before. It's not a bad thing, but don't get in trouble. If you need more cash to run your business, take the steps to get it.
- **Undercapitalized:** When you buy equipment for your rental fleet, it is important that you keep your company properly capitalized. If you are flush with cash, then use it. But if you are short on cash, the best solution may be to finance the purchase of rental boxes. We typically finance units that have already been purchased, and then put those into our rental fleet. This method gives us more control than having a lender pay our supplier directly for equipment going into our fleet.
- **Bad debt:** We all know companies that were slow payers during the good times, but in difficult economic times, more companies that never before struggled with cash flow can begin to struggle.

Cash Is King: Pay Attention to Your Cash-Flow Statement

ANDERS NORLIN

Good cash flow: What does it mean? Operating cash flow is what keeps your company afloat, but do you know what it means for your business? We all talk about the profitability of our companies and pay a lot of attention to the income statement and the balance sheet. However, the health of our businesses depends on the operating cash flow. There are two main reasons for why operating cash flow is a better measurement of a company's financial condition than net profit.

First, if your company can generate cash over the long term, it will prevail. Second, cash flow is more difficult to manipulate under the accounting rules than net income. Having negative cash flow is not necessarily bad if it is caused by investments in revenue generating assets, but it is detrimental if it means that the business is drained of its resources. In the financial world, the measurement "Earnings Before Interest Taxes Depreciation and Amortization" (EBITDA) is often referred to as the amount of cash a company generates. However, this measure does not capture changes in working capital (accounts receivables, inventories, etc.). Therefore, EBITDA really represents earnings before the effects of financing and capital investment. The true cash-flow measurement of your business is found in the statement of cash flows.

Overview of the Statement of Cash Flows

The statement of cash flows for most companies consists of three main parts.

- Cash flow from operating activities: This is the net cash generated from operations (net income and changes in working capital).
- Cash flow from investing activities: This is the net result of capital expenditures, investments, acquisitions, etc.
- Cash flow from financing activities: This refers to the net result of raising cash to fund the other flows or repaying debt.

The example below shows how the operating cash flow of a business is established by adjusting the current net profit with the changes of the balance sheet over the current period. Increases of assets, such as accounts receivable, and inventory and decreases of liabilities, such as accounts payable and loans, will reduce the amount of cash available. Decreases of the assets and increases of liabilities will increase the cash available. The current profit is also increased by reversing the amount of depreciation because it is a reduction of the value of assets and has no bearing on cash.

By taking net income and adjusting to reflect changes in the working capital accounts on the balance sheet (receivables, payables, inventories) and other current accounts, the operating cash-flow section shows how cash was generated or tied up during the period. It is this translation process from accrual accounting to cash accounting that makes the operating cash-flow statement so important.

Accrual Accounting vs. Cash Flows

The key differences between accrual accounting and real cash flow are demonstrated by the concept of the cash cycle. A company's cash cycle is the process that converts sales (based upon accrual accounting) into cash as follows:

1. Cash is used to make inventory.
2. Inventory is sold and converted into accounts receivable.
3. Cash is received when the customer pays.

There are many ways that cash from legitimate sales can get trapped on the balance sheet. The two most common occur when the customer delays payment, resulting in a build-up of receivables. It also causes a rise in inventory levels because the product is not selling as fast as planned, or product is being returned.

For example, a company might record a $20,000 sale, but because the customer pays in another fiscal period, the sale is not reflected on the income statement until the funds are received. If the payment occurs after the end of the fiscal year, accrued earnings will be greater than operating cash flow because the $20,000 is still showing as a receivable.

Manipulating Operating Cash Flows

Accrual accounting can give a rather provisional report of a company's profitability. It also provides management with a range of choices to record transactions. This flexibility is necessary, but it does allow for earnings manipulation. Because owners will generally book business in a way that will help the company either look good in the eyes of their banks or minimize profits for tax purposes, the income statement should always be compared to the cash-flow statement.

To increase sales, a company can book a sale of equipment before the customer has taken formal delivery. Inventories will then be reduced on the books and a sale will be recorded. Accrued earnings will increase, but the customer is not really committed to the purchase until the equipment is delivered or picked up. The earnings are therefore misleading. Assuming that the sale is consummated at a later date, this is simply a way to transfer earnings from one fiscal period to another. On the other hand, if units are held by a third party on consignment, and this is recorded as a sale, the earnings are clearly misrepresented.

The operating cash-flow statement will catch these manipulations. When operating cash flow is less than net income, there is something wrong with the cash cycle. In extreme cases, a company could have consecutive fiscal periods of negative operating cash flow. Suppliers, lenders, and shareholders should understand the source of the cash hemorrhage (inventories, receivables, etc.) and determine whether this situation is a short-term issue or a long-term problem.

Cash Exaggerations

While the operating cash-flow statement is more difficult to manipulate, there are ways for companies to temporarily boost cash flows. Some of the more common techniques include: delaying payment to suppliers (extending payables) and reversing charges made in prior quarters (such as restructuring reserves). Some view the selling of receivables for cash—usually at a discount—as a way for companies to manipulate cash flows. In some cases, this action may be a cash-flow manipulation, but it is also a legitimate financing strategy.

Cash Is King

A company can only live by good earnings alone for a limited time. Eventually, it will need cash to pay suppliers and, most importantly, the bankers. There are many examples of once-respected companies that went bankrupt because they could not generate enough cash. Usually this is due to rapid growth rather than slow times. Strangely, despite all the evidence, owners are consistently focused on the growth of sales, market momentum, and good earnings. As a result, they tend to overlook the signs of financial conditions visible in the statement of cash flows.

To Charge Sales Tax or Not: Pros and Cons

ANDERS NORLIN

In many states a portable storage operator can elect to pay either sales tax or use tax at the time he or she enters a container into the rental fleet. This avoids the obligation of charging sales tax to the rental customer. This selection enables the operator to offer a lower rental cost to the customer or charge the same rate as if sales tax was included while keeping the additional revenue. The selection may or may not be the best way to optimize profits. Here are some views of the pros and cons of the different methods.

The main argument I hear from companies that pay the use tax is that they can offer lower rates to their customers. I have even seen companies advertise the benefit that they don't charge sales tax. Obviously, the rate is a component of the cost. Theoretically, it should be a competitive advantage to not charge sales tax. However, one can argue that the amount is often insignificant and the typical quote is more or less always given without sales tax. Therefore, the buyer of rental service probably doesn't pay much attention to the fact that there is no sales tax charged.

The flip side of offering lower rates is to be able to charge the same rates as the competition, including sales tax. In other words, in an environment with an average sales tax of 8 percent, the company that selects the use tax method would obtain 8 percent more revenue than the competition with the same cost to the customer.

However, in this case, one is likely to have more challenges if the rental customer is shopping for good rates and compares one company over the other. The quote from a rental company that charges sales tax would be, for example, $80 per rental period and the quote from the company that doesn't charge sales tax would be $86.40 per rental period. Unless the customer asks the former operator for the cost including sales tax, the customer will see that the more expensive operator is the one who charges use tax.

There are also practical and financial considerations. On the practical side, the use tax operator has to keep track of sales and use taxes not only for the container, but also for other materials used to improve or up-fit the container. It is easy to pay use tax on the purchase cost of the container, which is usually purchased without sales tax from a trading or container leasing company. It is more complex to keep track of taxes paid on tools and materials that the operator may or may not be able to acquire with the exemption of sales tax. This may be offset if the operator does not have to file monthly or quarterly sales tax returns, which can be a tedious process. Secondly, if a container for which use tax is paid is sold, sales tax still applies unless the buyer is a reseller of containers. In other words, to handle the use tax method correctly, there are a lot of administrative tasks involved.

There are financial considerations. Paying use tax ties up capital. One should make a serious cost-benefit analysis comparing the cost of capital for each of the two methods. It doesn't seem like paying $160 in use tax on a $2,000 container is a big deal, but if one has a large fleet with five hundred units, then the amount is $80,000. That is equal to investing in an additional forty containers. Explained another way, for the use tax model to be beneficial, the operator must be able to increase the fleet by more than 8 percent as a result of offering a rate without sales tax, or charge the same rate as the competition, including sales tax, for an initial period that is 8 percent longer than the average rental term.

A third way to look at the use tax selection is to consider the number of rental periods it takes to recover the use tax. If the rental rate is $80 per rental period, the sales tax operator doesn't have to charge the extra $6.40; and if the use tax paid is $160, the recovery period is twenty-five rental periods. Furthermore, taking into consideration a utilization of 85 percent, the rental recovery period is twenty-nine rental periods, or two-and-a-half years. This is true as if the operator can charge the same amount as the customer would pay if the fee included paying sales tax.

- Market rental rate.................................$80.00
- Market rental rate including sales tax $86.40
- Container purchase cost........................ $2,000.00
- Use tax paid $160.00
- Monthly sales tax not being charged $6.40
- Recovery time in # of rental periods...... ($160/$6.40) 25

From my perspective, the largest negative of selecting the use tax model is what happens when the portable storage operator is looking to sell the business. In my article titled "Acquiring a Fleet of Portable Storage Containers On-Hire," published by the NPSA in December 2011, I discussed the different valuation models of a rental fleet.

One of the methods used for fleet and company evaluations is the "Return on Investment Method." These methods look at the cash-flow stream of a rental fleet and depending on the buyers' criteria for return on investment, he or she can establish a value of the fleet or business to be acquired. If the seller has selected the use tax model, the buyer can either pay sales tax on the fleet while maintaining the current status of the rental agreements or buy the fleet with the traditional sales tax model.

If the buyer chooses the traditional sales tax model, he or she is faced with rental agreements that are subject to sales tax. It is very difficult to maintain utilization, customer loyalty, and goodwill if one has to start charging sales tax and, therefore, make the customers pay more. For this reason, the buyer's best choice is to not charge sales tax to *current* customers and only charge sales tax for new rental agreements post-purchase. However, being faced with this situation, the buyer is going to require a discount from the seller in compensation for the lower rates. This discount is obviously related to the size of the sales tax, but it can still be a considerable amount. Here is an example:

- Annual rental revenue $884.00
- Buyer ROI requirement 25%
- Sale price per unit $3,536.00
- Use tax discount 8%

  –$283.00

- Discounted sale price $3,274.00
- Monthly sales tax not being charged $6.40
- Recovery time in # of rental periods ($283/$6.40) 44

We can also look at this from the perspective of how many rental periods it takes to recover the discount of the seller's selection of the use tax method. In the example above, that period amounts to forty-four rental periods, which is about three-and-a-half years.

A portable storage operator can elect to pay use tax on containers, which avoids having to charge customers for sales tax. The challenges with selecting this method are:

- The customers are used to quotes being made exclusive of sales tax and therefore tend to overlook the benefit of the method.
- The operator will have a competitive disadvantage if his quotes are made at the same price as a competitor using the traditional sales tax method including sales tax.

- The administration of add-on expenses and capital improvements to the containers can be complex.
- The use tax is a cash layout that has to be recovered over an extended period of time either by higher rates, longer rental periods, or an increased number of customers.
- The use tax method has a negative impact on the valuation of a rental fleet and a seller of such a fleet cannot expect the same price as if the traditional sales tax method was used.

If you are using the use tax method, I recommend that you look at the benefits of converting to a sales tax model, especially if you are looking to sell your business within the next few years. Secondly, do very detailed calculations if you are considering this method. Obviously, all markets aren't the same; rates and sales tax rates may differ and therefore the choice of method can be more or less beneficial.

Dealing with Slow Payers

PHIL HERNDON

I have a rental customer who has been a slow payer for four years. I have visited the company, called the staff, and sent letters and faxes asking for payment. I have even offered a discount for paying on time. Still, they are typically sixty or more days behind. It's wild. They seem to plan on paying late. But I'd rather have them as a customer than not at all. It's a little more work, but it can be managed.

It's the unknown slow payers that can be the real problem. There are $100 invoices that haven't been paid for three months.

Dealing with slow payers starts in your office. Each Monday after the Saturday checks are entered, I download an accounts receivable list and then remove anyone who is inside of fifty-nine days. We print two copies of the list and review it with our receivable clerk and, as needed, the rest of the office staff. The discipline of doing this has an amazing impact. I take notes, review the previous week's report and notes, and celebrate our successes or redouble our efforts on the difficult accounts. Of course, we look at all receivables, but we start with the sixty-day and overs first.

Even the best businesses will have to cope with some deadbeats. This is the customer whose voicemail has reached its message capacity. So, you visit your container. It's behind a fence and the gate is locked. How do you handle this situation?

Be a nice guy, assume the best, but don't be lazy! Leave a polite note asking for a call and attach it to the gate lock. Visit the neighbors, politely ask about the customer, but make sure people know you are concerned about your rental equipment.

I had one of these customers recently at a residence. No one answered the door of the house, so I went to the neighbors. They explained that the family was going through a time of hardship. So, I went back, knocked on the door again, and waited until a woman answered. We talked. I mentioned the outstanding bill and the phone messages we had left, and then I asked her to tell me what was happening. Did she really need the container? Could she pay the bill?

As we talked I learned she was working nights, her husband was on disability, the house belonged to her son, and the container held their life possessions. Although my reputation is anything but soft, I asked her what level of monthly payment would be acceptable for her. She suggested a reasonable amount, agreed to clean up the amount past due and to stay current. I felt good knowing I was helping the family in a time of need. Their account is back in good standing. But I'd feel better if this was the norm.

Let's say you've exhausted the nice guy approach and have to turn up the heat. The phone calls aren't returned, no one knows where the customer is, and another month goes by. You call your buddy who's an attorney. Mine lets me write a letter that he prints on his letterhead and sends. It's a cannon shot over the bow to get some attention. A sample:

Dear Mr. Slow Pay,
I have been retained by Container Solutions in the matter of storage containers rented to you and currently on your property. Unfortunately, as detailed in the enclosed statement, invoices since July have not been paid. Additionally, I understand from my client that there has been no response to his efforts to communicate with your company about ways to resolve this.

Please respond to our client so that this situation can be resolved in an agreeable manner for both parties. Should you not be willing to work directly with Container Solutions, we will have no choice but to begin legal action against your company for payment and recovery of the equipment. If my client has not heard from you within ten days, please know that our firm will be in contact with you.

We've had some success with these letters. If there is no response, then it's time to really roll up your sleeves or call the professionals!

Over-Lock

This involves going to the customer's location and installing an additional lock on the container. You can use a high security lock that attaches to the lock rods, a heavy chain that secures the doors, or any method that prevents the customer from opening the doors.

I have talked to several operators who consider this the most effective method for getting a customer to bring their account current.

There are several NPSA associate members who provide excellent products for this. Once you have locked out a customer, it's a good idea to let them know with a letter and phone call. Acknowledge the inconvenience it may cause when you let them know they have left you with no choice.

Repossession

The process for repossession varies significantly from state to state, so please investigate this locally before you act. Your rental contract means everything in one state and nothing in another. If you don't like to pay for legal counsel, try chatting with a local contractor's equipment rental company and a mini storage operator. Between the two of them, you'll get an idea of how the repossession and disposal of goods for portable storage should be handled.

Before a civil court can provide a writ of repossession (aka: writ of replevin), you must prove that you have exhausted all reasonable methods of collection or repossession. This can be done by showing notes, letter copies, or anything that shows you have, for a reasonable period, been pursuing the customer for payment. Additionally, the judge will ask for proof of ownership and a signed rental contract. If you are using a collector or repossessor, those agents will provide an affidavit of due diligence, proving that they have exhausted all collection efforts.

When the judge issues the writ of repossession then you are in a position to enlist law enforcement to facilitate access to the property and repossession of your equipment. Some states require a recovery agent to complete the physical task of repossession.

Online information can be helpful, but most sources address vehicle repossession.

I am sure that many of you are reading this and saying, "I'll just go get my container. I don't need a judge or a sheriff to help me!" Yes, you can do that, especially since the rental customer would have little resource to fight you for trespassing or taking their possessions inside the storage container.

Personal Property

There have been times when we pushed out all the contents in our container, loaded the container on our truck, and headed on down the road. You could also bring the container back to your yard, cut the lock, and open it up. It's anybody's guess what you'll find inside. We had one that was full of commercial sprinkler fittings. After trying the local flea market and Craigslist we hauled it all to the dump! I have heard stories of operators finding grandma's wedding dress, a priceless collection of comic books, and so on; but we have yet to find contents that could be sold for anything close to the total amount owed. One NPSA member said he found airplane wings inside a repossessed container, which was cool, but not easy to sell.

As a rule, you must notify the customer of your intent to sell the customer's belongings. I have heard of waiting periods ranging from thirty to ninety days. Be willing to compromise. Save yourself the hassle of trying to do better at an auction, flea market, or on the Internet. Be aware that if the sale value of the goods exceeds what is owed to you (past rent, recovery, and storage costs) you may be required to return the excess amount to the customer.

Liens

Using the lien process can be another method to get paid. In this case, you file a document that prevents significant change to the debtor's property without your claim being settled. We have filed a lien against a property owner after we received a small claims court judgment in our favor only to find there were seven other liens filed against the same property. After five years, we still hadn't seen any money. Results depend on how the property owner feels about a lien. If your customer is renting the property where your container resides or did reside, the landlords are usually very motivated to make their tenant settle your claim so that they don't have to fight the lien's validity.

Lien services that take care of filing can be found online. We just work through the local county recorder's office. It is not a difficult process.

Don't let the vilification of collections hold you back from being effective. Debt collection and recovery of your property does not require you to get upset, be heartless, or threaten people. Just set up a company policy and follow that. What you don't collect effects your bottom line. Time is not your friend when clients owe you money!

New Tools for Collections: Better Cash Flow and Less Administration

ANDERS NORLIN

Our world is becoming more and more mobile with electronic transactions taking place at all levels of the business chain. Collecting payments at the "point of sale" used to be possible only by retail outlets. Today, a payment at the "point of sale" can be made anywhere there is cell phone coverage. This is an instant, simple, secure, and affordable process that improves service.

In the "good old days," your driver would pick up a check from the customer upon delivering a portable storage container for rental or sale. The check then had to be delivered to the bank. Sometimes the bank would place a hold on checks from questionable accounts. Today, with the right tools, the check can be processed into an electronic payment that is credited to your bank account and entered into your accounting system instantaneously at the delivery site.

Mobile Credit Card Readers

There are several systems available for instant payments. The most commonly used is the credit or debit card. It's not a recent phenomenon, but what's new is the ability to collect the payment and issue a receipt to the payee via your smart phone. The ideal solution is to have an app that can integrate the payment with your accounting systems and issue an electronic receipt to the payee.

QuickBooks seems to be the most commonly used accounting system in our industry. Intuit offers a product for credit card payments called GoPayment that attaches to your iPhone or Android phone. You can subscribe to this service with a monthly subscription fee and a minimum transaction fee, or you can use it as needed by paying a higher transaction fee. The fees range from 1.75 percent to 3.75 percent of the transaction amount. Although this is an added expense, your collection is completed and accounted for with the swipe of a credit card at the point of sale. If you go this route, make sure you select a product that protects the payee's credit card number. There are regulations that stipulate the use and storage of credit card numbers. Most major vendors have addressed this issue, but you want to make sure that you are protected from employee misuse or from others who might find your lost or stolen phone.

Remote Check Collection

Remote check collection is a service that allows you to take a picture of a check and deposit it in your bank account. More and more banks have apps for this service. If your bank doesn't offer remote check collection yet, look into using PayPal's phone app. PayPal acts as an intermediary between your smart phone and your bank account.

Using remote deposit is quite easy. You endorse the check you receive from your customer and then use your smartphone to take a picture of the front and back of the check. The banking app will make sure you have a quality snapshot and then send it to the bank. Some banks will give you instant access to the funds while others will make you wait for the funds to clear. If you set up this function for your drivers, make sure they are limited to only making deposits to your bank account. You don't want to give them additional features, such as seeing balances or making payments and transfers.

Collection of Payment via ACH

ACH stands for Automated Clearing House. It is an electronic network for financial transactions within the United States. Most banks offer this system to their commercial customers. Having ACH capabilities allows you (the vendor) to access your customer's bank account and withdraw funds. ACH is a very practical way to collect reoccurring payments and lends itself well to a portable storage rental company. Using ACH services requires some documentation between the vendor and his customer. Typically, that is done with an ACH agreement that authorizes the vendor to withdraw funds, specifies the customer's bank ABA number, and identifies the customer's bank account number. The agreement can be very specific regarding frequency, amounts, days of withdrawal, and the term of the agreement. It can also be very generic, authorizing the vendor to collect funds in general. I recommend that you have a clause in your standard rental agreement that authorizes you to do generic collections via ACH.

It is understandable that customers are concerned with a generic authorization, but they are well-protected by the vendor's bank, which is required to adhere to the rules of NACHA (The Electronic Payments Association) and the Federal Reserve Bank. These rules make the vendor's bank put a limit on what can be collected by the client. If there is unauthorized use of the services by the vendor, the collecting bank is responsible to reverse incorrect collections. Dealing with a dispute is as easy as objecting to an incorrect credit card charge or putting a stop on a check.

Renting portable storage containers is increasingly competitive. The industry figured out a long time ago that service, not price, is the way to win customers. Therefore, using new solutions to make the business process easier and faster for the customer, and simplifying administrative routines is a way to stay ahead of the competition.

Small Claims Court

PHIL HERNDON

We had then customers who clearly were not going to pay us. Two of the customers still had our rental containers but the rest did not. We proceeded with small claims on all ten of them. Here is the process:

1. **Fill out the small claims form and file it with the court.** Do multiple cases at the same time, that way your cases will be heard on the same day, one right after the other. For us, the cost is $30 per claim up to $1500, and $50 per claim for amounts ranging from $1500-$5000. Those fees apply if you have not filed more than twelve claims in a twelve-month period. Read the application form well. You'll need to bring extra copies of some documents or pay the court for copies.
2. **Hire a process server to find and serve each debtor.** Do this right after you file the claim; it is time-critical that the defendant (debtor) be served within a reasonable time before the trial. If the server has found the debtor, they will file an affidavit of proof of service. In our case, the process server could only locate six of the ten debtors. Costs vary. For us, the fee was $75 to $100 per case, depending on the location.
3. **Show up for court.** Bring with you all back-up documentation. This might include contracts, copies of invoices, statements, notes on collection calls, and pictures of the storage unit at the debtor's location. Small claims court is an interesting experience. Once all the formalities of bringing the court into session are completed, the judge will review the docket of cases. In my case, none of the defendants appeared to defend themselves. The judge figured that out and so called me up. We quickly went through each case. None were contested, so the judge asked no questions and did not ask for any proof of claim. He said he'd rule and mail his decision to me shortly. Within a week, I received his rulings, all in our favor.

4. **We then turned the cases over to a judgement collection firm.** These companies will typically have you sign documents that assign the judgement to their company with the provision that any funds collected would be shared at an agreed rate. In our case, the rate was 50 percent. Six weeks passed, and we still had not received a nickel, but I remained confident that the collection firm had a better chance to collect on our claim than we had.

As we waited for payment of some kind, I considered the cost and time involved. My only justification is knowing that we did all we could to get the customer to pay. Some would argue that a regular bill collector would be a wiser option. After twenty years of trying more than six different collection companies, we have not found this to be effective.

In comparison to other industries, portable storage has a very low percentage of bad debt. That low ratio can be attributed to several factors, but we need to focus on those factors that we can control. Managing your receivables is critical to your success.

Do You Have the Capital You Need to Grow?

ANDERS NORLIN

The portable storage industry is growing, the economy is strong, rental rates and equipment prices are on the rise. To be prepared for growth, look into the possibility of obtaining capital from different sources: banks, leasing companies, state and federal programs, as well as investors and your own untapped assets.

Growth in the portable storage industry requires capital. For each new container on-hire, the capital outlay is somewhere between $1,000 and $3,000, depending on equipment type, company location, and improvements made to the container. Another challenge is timing. Do you have capital available when equipment prices are low or opportunities present themselves? Take a moment and reflect on the growth of your container rental fleet during any recent year. How much money would you have saved if your purchases for the year had been made from January to March instead of April to August? This is a seasonal business. Prices are lower when containers are off-hire during the winter and early spring. Prices are higher when containers are on-hire during the late spring, summer, and fall.

Nevertheless, most rental companies purchase equipment when they have a customer rather than when container prices are low. It is a more conservative approach to purchase when you have a customer, but what is the cost you pay for being conservative? For example, let's say you buy a container for $1,500 in January instead of $1,800 in May. Using an interest rate of 9 percent, the cost of owning the $1,500 unit for the period January through April is 3 percent of $1,500, or $45, while your price increase was $300. Quite a difference!

Be prepared for growth and be prepared to take advantage of purchasing opportunities by contacting potential funding sources long before you have the need for capital. Here is a list of different types of lenders.

Banks

The most obvious place to seek additional capital is from your bank. Make sure you have a relationship with the bankers long before you need to borrow money. Meet regularly with your local branch manager. Explain your business, how your company operates, and how you expect to grow. If you do not already have a loan, get a small credit line. If necessary, secure it with cash and use it actively over six to nine months so that you establish a credit history.

Equipment Leasing Companies

Lease financing differs from bank financing in several ways. First, the financing is earmarked for specific equipment. Second, lease financing is typically for 100 percent of the equipment value whereas bank financing most often requires some equity participation from the borrower.

State Government Programs

Portable storage companies generate jobs, such as drivers, mechanics, and administrative staff. Most states have small business financing programs for companies that create job opportunities. Check with your secretary of state.

Federal Government Programs

The Small Business Administration (SBA) provides guarantees to your bank for up to 80 percent of the loan principal. In particular, the 7(a) Loan Program is suitable for portable storage companies. It provides a long-term, fixed-rate loan for equipment. SBA is not a lender, but if you qualify for their program, SBA will provide a guarantee to your bank. To find out more, talk to your local banker about SBA or visit *www.sba.gov*. For a company that experiences rapid growth, it may be more advantageous to invite investors to provide capital rather than to borrow money. Although the owner has to give up a share of the company, knowing one or several professional investors, in the long run, can be far more valuable than the shares the owner has given up.

Small Business Investment Companies

SBICs are investment firms licensed by the SBA to provide equity investments and long-term loans to small companies. To find out more, visit *www.sba.gov/inv.*

Angel Investors

An angel investor is someone who invests in a business expansion either through debt or equity financing at a very early stage of growth. A typical "angel" is a wealthy individual, a supplier with interest in the growth, or a customer who needs the company as a solid supplier of services.

If none of these alternatives is a way for you to find capital, you can look to your own untapped sources. The options you have for finding more money in your own backyard are often limited, but here are some alternatives.

Home Equity Financing

If your home has unused equity, use it for your business. Just be sure to invest in good equipment that generates steady income and doesn't lose its value. This is one of the better and most inexpensive ways to finance an expansion. A key question is, how many containers can you buy with this money?

Retirement Plans

Do you have money in an IRA or a 401(k) plan? If so, you might consider converting it into a loan to your company by creating a self-governed trust. To find out more, visit *http://www.sterling-trust.com/* and talk to your CPA.

Friends and Family Members

As a last resort, you may want to borrow money from friends and family. Most often, this is an easy way, but it has pitfalls. First, financial matters can be very difficult to deal with when friends and family are involved. Second, this category of lender is not going to scrutinize your loan proposal as thoroughly as a professional lender, which may lead to unrealistic expectations and cause conflict.

Most likely, you will approach several different sources and explore what is best suited for your situation. Make sure you have done your homework and can present a viable case. Here is a list of materials that you will need.

- Two years of financial statements
- Professionally prepared financial and cash flow projections
- A market, industry, and company presentation
- The owner's personal financial statements
- The background and resumes of the owner and key management

Be realistic. It takes time for a lender or investor to evaluate your application. Unless you have an established relationship, a financing process can take six months or more. Therefore, be proactive; contact your prospective lenders and investors early so that you have the funds available when the prices are right and the equipment is available.

Reoccurring Revenue

PHIL HERNDON

In fifth grade, I was nearly expelled for refusing to write an essay on the greatest invention of all time. It was ridiculous to suggest that there was one invention that was the greatest. In protest, I wrote about the invention of the sewing machine. Obviously, I was never the teacher's pet. Despite that childhood experience, and inspired by the 1991 movie *City Slickers* to identify one thing to work for, here is the "just one thing" to help you run your business.

Passive income is that wonderful phenomenon with which you continue to receive income with almost no effort on your part to maintain incoming cash flow. Any single-site operator with a rental fleet knows what this is. Opening checks from rental customers is one of the most enjoyable things a business owner can do! Passive income is my "one thing" award.

In 1999 when I started my company, I was just selling containers. That was profitable, and I did well. But like most things in life, the easy route is not the best one. I had wonderful relationships and good sales, but I was only as good as my last sale. If the phone did not ring or if equipment dried up, I was out of luck and broke. After five years of selling containers, I began renting boxes.

Our rental fleet has become a great source of revenue. We enjoy those twenty-eight-day payments. For years, I have asked: "Show me another business where someone pays you to place your company billboard on their property!" The only thing better would be an appreciating asset that provides passive income, such as commercial property or a ministorage. If you compare those two options, the advantages depend on the owner's preferences and capital resources.

Portable Storage	Rental	Mini-Storage
Asset Appreciation	None	Yes
Start-Up Costs	Low	High
Service Area	Variable	Fixed
Customer Payment Risk	Medium-Low	Low
Overhead	Low	Medium
Tax Exposure	Medium	Medium
Exit Plan	Easy Sell	Easy Sell

When it comes to portable storage, what could go wrong with this golden goose of passive income?

1. **Future generations could be less interested in owning things.** Imagine a society in which we did not need to own so much stuff. That would not only impact the people who get paid to store things, but also the manufacturers who make the stuff and the supply chain that moves the stuff. Almost a doomsday scenario! Thankfully, a shift like this would take many decades to fully impact us.
2. **A more competitive product could replace portable self-storage.** We might think that it would be difficult for this to happen, but we can see how mobile self-storage quickly came into the space that existed between portable self-storage and mini-storage. For most of us (or maybe just me), it took a few years to understand this industry. We could have done a better job of understanding customer needs.
3. **Change is inevitable.** We can't hold onto what works today with any confidence that it will work tomorrow.

Risk and the inevitability of change exist for any business venture, but on a comparative basis, portable self-storage is not a bad way to make a living! As I type, I am reminded that my post office box is being stuffed with rental payments! What a wonderful feeling, and a real "one thing"!

The Credit Crunch: What It Is and What It Means

ANDERS NORLIN

Do you know what a so-called "credit crunch" means? Let's look more closely at economic periods when there is a credit crunch and how it might impact your business.

Change in Terms, Conditions, and Requirements

A credit crunch (also known as a credit squeeze or credit crisis) is a rapid reduction in the general availability of loans (or credit), or a stringent tightening of the conditions required to obtain a loan from banks and other traditional lenders. A credit crunch generally occurs independent of changes in official interest rates.

In other words, a credit crunch can make it more difficult to borrow money for reasons other than interest costs. In these situations, the relationship between credit availability and interest rates have changed so that credit becomes less available and/or there ceases to be a clear relationship between interest rates and credit availability (i.e. credit rationing). Typically, a credit crunch also means a change in the types of loans a bank or an investor is prepared to give. In addition to looking at the "risk/reward" relationship, lenders look more closely at the "quality" of the borrower.

Traditionally, that means that lenders favor larger companies with a long and stable track record. They pull away from opportunities to maximize the return on their investments or to provide more credit to the market. Furthermore, lenders do more to scrutinize loans for business expansion. Lending for current documented needs is more comforting than investment in machinery, tools, or marketing efforts.

In simple terms, a credit crunch is a reduction of fuel for the economy. You may need credit and have the means to pay for it, but it isn't available because the terms and conditions for borrowing have changed. The changes can be major (i.e. your industry may have fallen out of favor), or, in a better-case scenario, you are required to provide a higher portion of equity relative to the amount you want to borrow. There have been times when we saw debt-to-equity

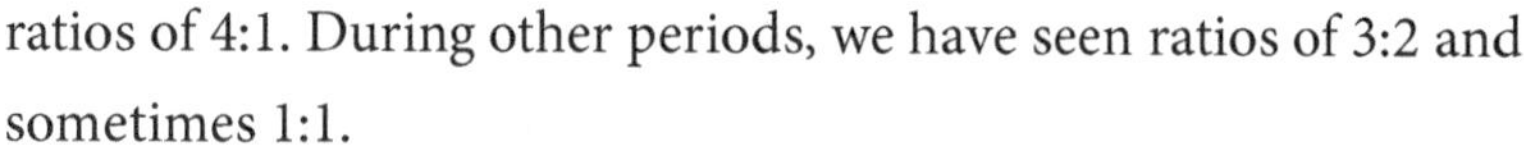

ratios of 4:1. During other periods, we have seen ratios of 3:2 and sometimes 1:1.

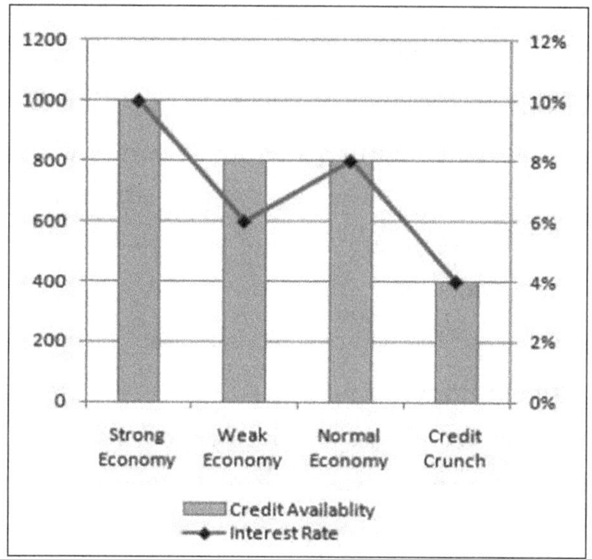

Credit Is Just Another Product

Credit is a product provided by banks and investors, so it follows the traditional rules of supply and demand. The more that borrowers are prepared to pay in the form of interest (the price), the more credit (the product) is available. The less demand there is for the product, the lower the price charged by banks and investors.

A credit crunch redefines these rules. First, the amounts available to the borrowers are decreased. Second, it increases borrowing requirements and thereby limits the number of qualified customers, which reduces aggregate demand. Therefore, there is a lower *pro rata* share of borrowers is in the market and the price (the interest rate) of the product (the credit) is reduced.

The table above illustrates how the interest rate and supply of credit changes in typical economic cycles. For simplicity's sake, the typical economies are defined as strong, weak, and normal. In those three situations, there is a logical relationship between the amount of credit available and the interest rate. In a credit crunch scenario, the volume of available credit is reduced because the market for the credit has shrunk as a result of higher requirements on the borrower. The interest rate drops because it is more difficult to attract qualified customers. The interest rate may also be down because the qualified borrowers are reluctant to borrow when the economy is in a depressed stage.

How a Credit Crunch Happens

A credit crunch is often caused by a sustained period of careless and inappropriate lending, which results in losses for lenders and investors. The carelessness refers to overinflated asset values, overly positive expectations of growth, and the hyper-optimism that comes with a rapid expansion.

Once the optimism and expectation start to change, the view of values and opportunities change from positive to negative. When losses start to appear, the degree of loss accelerates as bad news feeds on itself. Therefore, lenders and investors become increasingly prudent and restrictive. The prudence and restrictions reflect the loss of confidence among lenders and investors in the economy for the near future.

In times like this, one often hears, "Rule number one is not to lose money; rule number two is to make money." If the sentiment is, "I am better off holding my money than lending it or investing it," then economic growth slows down. If the credit crunch is so severe that banks and investors pull back credit that is already performing, then the economy slows down. Healthy businesses can suddenly find themselves without the capital they need to operate.

Credit is a necessary part of business. Most companies have some kind of credit facility, such as a credit line with a bank or terms with its vendors. One can say that credit is like oil in a car; you don't think much about it, but when it isn't there you have big problems. For example, a portable storage company that is financing its fleet of rental containers with a credit line would have a major problem if the credit line was suddenly terminated.

Credit lines typically have a one-year term and are often renewed without any major issues (provided the customer is doing well and paying the interest). Banks can decide to remove credit lines that are renewed annually. If that happens, the rental company is forced to find financing elsewhere. This can be a monumental task in a restrictive credit environment. The other alternative to paying off the credit line is to sell part of the rental fleet to generate cash. This will hurt more than help the company in the long run.

During the 2007-2008 financial crisis, we experienced one of the most difficult economic situations since the Great Depression, World War II, the oil crisis of the 1970s, or the inflationary times of the early 1980s. The challenges presented during those downturns where overcome one way or another. But we rarely hear much about opportunities that present themselves during downturns. Slowly but surely, opportunities emerge and lenders become less restrictive. During downturns it will help if you to stay in close contact with your banker. Show him or her your business and talk about the opportunities you see. Bankers are, after all, business professionals. It is their job to lend money.

Making investments in bad times is usually good strategy. The trick is to invest in the right kind of opportunity. If you are in the portable storage business, look at what your business needs today. There are bargains to be made in buying trucks, trailers, lifts, tools, and other machinery. Check the local newspaper listings and the Internet for distressed sales and talk to others in your local business community about your needs. I say "needs" because downturns can be a great time for buying what you need and not buying everything you think you can use.

Taking advantage of opportunities doesn't exclude being prudent. If you don't need it, don't buy it. But buy it if you need it, when the price is right. If you feel comfortable with the long-term strategy of your company, a downturn is a great time to build your infrastructure. Have you had another yard or expansion of your existing facilities in mind? Perhaps an economic valley is the time to look for real estate deals. Talk to your realtor and local banker about what's available in your neighborhood. Banks, accountants, and bankruptcy lawyers often sit on valuable information concerning things that are about to happen. With a few phone calls, you'll find out what is going on in your area that isn't common knowledge. Those may be some of the most profitable calls you ever make.

Put Your Retirement Money to Work in Your Business!

ANDERS NORLIN

Many of us think it is better to invest retirement money in something other than our own businesses. Therefore, we have no choice but to leave the funds with a financial advisor or CPA because the rules for retirement funds are complex. We understand that advisors are heavily regulated and therefore invest our funds mostly in public stocks or bonds. Have you asked yourself where your funds are best invested? Have you considered investing your retirement money in your own business?

Not many people do this, but there are ways to invest your 401(k) or other qualified retirement plan in your own business without being hit with taxes and early withdrawal penalties. Most financial advisors steer customers away from these types of solutions. They argue that small businesses are risky investments and we should diversify.

However, as an entrepreneur, I am willing to take risks. If the money is invested in my own company, I can make diversifications myself. In addition, I don't have to invest all of my retirement funds in my business. Moreover, investments in real estate and stock are not risk-free! Many investments in financial instruments are destined to fail when advisors pursue their personal wealth instead of acting on behalf of their clients.

Prior to the housing market's collapse, entrepreneurs typically took out a second mortgage on their homes to finance business ventures. As property values dwindled across the country, so did the ability of small business owners to raise capital. Clearly, retirement accounts are an untapped source. It comes in handy for all small business owners but particularly for those in the start-up mode or those making substantial investments.

There are two ways to proceed (one less complex than the other). The first solution is to establish a 401(k) plan in your business and transfer the money from your original retirement plan to the 401(k). The funds in the 401(k) can then be borrowed for business purposes. However, there are some restrictions. The loans are limited to $50,000 and cannot be more than 50 percent of the 401(k)'s value. Furthermore, the loan must be amortized over five years and interest must be paid in the range of 1 percent to 2 percent above prime. Depending on how large your business is, $50,000 may or may not be a substantial amount; but if you can use that amount for buying and selling containers, it can be a meaningful addition to the bottom line.

Here is an example. If you buy containers for $50,000 and can resell them with a 20 percent markup, then you have made $10,000. Now, let's say that you pay cash to your vendor and your customer pays cash to you. If it takes thirty days from when you buy the containers until they are sold, then you can turn your inventory twelve times per year. That's an addition to the bottom line of $120,000 less interest.

Most likely, establishing a 401(k) and using the funds this way beats the return in your traditional retirement account. As long as you use the funds for activities that generate immediate cash, this solution works well. If you use the money for longer term investments then you have to think about the net cash flow after taxes, interest, and amortization. If the loans are not paid promptly, the unpaid portion is subject to income tax and penalties, if the owner is younger than fifty-nine-years old.

The second method is called ROBS, Roll Over as Business Startups. This arrangement enables a business owner to convert retirement accounts into business capital by using the rollover process. By creating a new corporation that sponsors a new retirement plan, the individual can rollover funds from a prior retirement account into the new plan. Then, through an exchange of corporate stock for the roll-over money, the owner receives instant business capital.

The retirement plan owns all the stock for the benefit of the owner, and the business receives needed cash. The plan has created a new owner of the corporation, which is the retirement account. The beneficiary is the owner of the retirement account. The benefit of this plan is that all funds are made available; there are no restrictions on amounts, there is no limit on how long the funds can be used.

However, there are several challenges with the ROBS plan. First, to establish the stock price, the value of the business must be confirmed by an independent appraiser. Second, the IRS (at least in the past) has been unclear on a number of issues concerning the ROBS plan. One important concern is that the distribution restrictions normally associated with taking money out of a retirement plan are circumvented. Another is that the capital (which includes previously untaxed income) is deferred while the owner of the retirement account benefits from the use of the capital. Another concern is that the new retirement account is only beneficial for the business owner and doesn't include the employees of the new company (which is technically the purpose of a retirement plan). Most owners don't want their employees to have stock in their company and therefore they close the retirement fund once it has been set up and the capital has been invested. In addition, there are a number of companies that can help set up a ROBS. However, if the fees are paid with funds from the retirement account, the fund may be in breach of IRS regulations.

So, as you think about where to get more capital, your retirement accounts may be a source. Do you want to risk using your retirement funds? If you are confident in your business, that could make sense, especially if you don't use all your retirement savings. Because the IRS rulings might not be clear, there could be a noncommercial risk. Finally, the tax rules are complex and how they apply varies from one situation to another; therefore, be sure to have good tax advice before you establish any of these programs.

Lease Finance Your Trucks and Spend Your Cash on Containers

ANDERS NORLIN

Leasing trucks is an option for business owners who have limited capital or who need trucks that must be upgraded every few years.

Each business owner's situation is unique and the decision to buy or lease must be made on a case-by-case basis. However, for a company in the portable storage business, it seems that leasing trucks is the better option. Let's compare the two options.

Advantages of Leasing Trucks

Leasing business trucks preserves capital and provides the flexibility of buying or returning the vehicles at the end of the lease. However, it may cost you more in the long run. The primary advantage of leasing business trucks is that it allows you to acquire tools that are critical to your business with minimal initial expenditures. Because truck leases require a limited down payment, you can obtain the trucks you need without significantly affecting your cash flow.

Another financial benefit of leasing trucks is that your lease payments can usually be deducted as business expenses on your tax return, reducing the net cost of your lease. In addition, leases are usually easier to obtain and have more flexible terms than loans for buying trucks. This can be a significant advantage if you have questionable credit or need to negotiate a longer payment plan to lower your payments.

Leasing also allows businesses to address the problem of obsolescence or upgrades required by environmental regulations. Certain leasing programs include service maintenance and replacement vehicles which make it easy to project costs and assure that your trucks are always available for use.

Finally, leasing trucks provides you with newer trucks with higher reliability and better appearance, which enhances the image of your business vis-a-vis the customer.

Disadvantages of Leasing Trucks

Leasing business trucks has two main disadvantages: overall cost and lack of ownership. With regard to cost, leasing an item is almost always more expensive than purchasing it. It is a form of rental and the benefits of leasing have to be weighed against the alternative use of your capital. For instance, if you have $50,000 in cash, you can buy a truck or buy containers for your rental fleet—containers that can go out on-rent almost immediately. In this case, leasing is the better choice. But if you have excess containers sitting around and no immediate demand for renting them out, then purchasing the truck is the better option.

Leases can be inflexible and are not easy to cancel. Most often you are penalized if you decide to terminate the lease prior to its termination date and the penalties can be as much as the total of the remaining lease payments.

Finally, there are very few lease programs for second-hand trucks; therefore, leasing instead of buying limits your opportunity to acquire good second-hand trucks.

Advantages of Buying Trucks

Ownership and tax breaks make buying business trucks appealing, but high initial cash payments mean that this option isn't for everyone. The most obvious advantage of buying business trucks is that, after you purchase the trucks, you gain ownership of them. This is especially true when the truck has a long, useful life and can be used in your business for a long period of time.

Tax incentives are another reason to consider purchasing business trucks. At the time of this writing, section 179 of the Internal Revenue Code allows you to accelerate the depreciation of some newly purchased assets in the first year. The benefit of section 179 varies between years, but it has been as high as 100 percent. In other words, if you bought a truck for $50,000, you could have taken depreciation in the same amount in one year. This is obviously helpful if you have large variations in your income year over year.

Although not all truck purchases are eligible for section 179 treatment, you can still receive tax savings for almost any business trucks through depreciation deductions.

Disadvantages of Buying Trucks

For some companies, purchasing business trucks may not be an option because the initial cash outlay is too high. Even if you plan on borrowing the money and making monthly payments, most banks require a down payment of around 20 percent. Borrowing money may also tie up lines of credit, and lenders may place restrictions on your future financial operations to ensure that you are able to repay your loan.

Although ownership is perhaps the biggest advantage to buying business trucks, it can also be a disadvantage. If you purchase, you run the risk that the trucks may become technologically obsolete or, for environmental reasons, become excessively costly to operate. This may force you to reinvest in new trucks long before you had intended. And you would need to sell the old ones at bargain prices.

Buy or Lease?

When deciding whether to buy or lease business trucks, you should try to figure out the approximate net cost of that asset. Be sure to factor in tax breaks and resale value when making this calculation. Furthermore, compare your costs to the alternative use of your capital.

For portable storage businesses, leasing trucks seems like a better alternative than buying trucks because the return on investment in containers is typically much higher than the cost of capital for a truck lease.

Improve the Bottom Line: Revenue and Expense Details

ANDERS NORLIN

At the time of this writing, the US economy has been growing steadily. Most portable storage companies have seen their fleet and profitability grow at a healthy rate. However, it is likely that the growth rate will decline a bit. Fine-tuning your ancillary charges, damage waiver, fuel surcharge, cleaning, content insurance, etc., will help you optimize revenues without increasing the investment in storage containers.

Another way to improve the bottom line is, obviously, to trim costs. This is something easily done by being more efficient.

Increasing Revenues

Improving results comes from reducing costs and increasing revenues, the latter being more exciting than the former. In the portable storage industry, increasing revenue most often comes from increasing the rental fleet, which means increasing the need for capital. The effort takes time and can be challenging. Another avenue for increasing revenue is obviously to increase what you can collect from your existing rental fleet in the form of fees.

Billing Periods: Traditionally, our industry uses a twenty-eight-day billing period, which allows for thirteen billing periods in one year. However, some companies are still using the historical calendar month billing and therefore forego 8 percent of their rent potential. For those companies, an instant switch of billing periods will make a significant improvement to the bottom line. That there will be customer complaints is understandable. One can expect a minimal loss of customers. On the other hand, the overall improvement of the rental revenue in the long run offsets the negative reactions and loss of a few customers.

A subtler way to switch from monthly to twenty-eight-day billing is obviously to set a date after which all new customers are on a twenty-eight-day billing cycle. Depending on your billing system's capacity, this method can be challenging.

Fuel Surcharges: The typical ancillary charges are fuel surcharges and damage waivers, which the customer typically accepts or at least has become accustomed to accepting. When the cost of oil and fuel is low, the fuel surcharge may be challenged by customers. Earn goodwill by being proactive and lowering your fuel surcharges; it should pay off in the long run.

Damage Waiver: The damage waiver is a profitable ancillary service offered to the customer. From the customer's perspective, it is insurance that protects him or her from charges for damages to the rented container. Typically, the damage waiver fee is a percentage of the rental costs. However, one could use another formula for the damage waiver fee and thereby increase revenues. The cost basis of the damage waiver fee could be the average cost of containers or the average cost of damages. As long as it is well-presented, customers are likely to accept the fee.

Cleaning Fee: Containers get dirty while out on-hire and should be cleaned before being presented to the next customer.

Charging a cleaning fee and taking responsibility for the cleaning, both exterior and interior, means that you have control of the quality of the cleaning. You have also created another revenue source. Most customers consider this a convenience and will not object to the fee.

Content Insurance: Damage to a container's contents can be an issue. It is beneficial for both the customer and the operator if the customer has insured the contents. Content insurance should be offered through a bona fide insurance carrier. Self-insuring, as most operators typically do for the damage waiver, is too risky.

Trimming Expenses

The other side of the coin is reducing your costs. Trimming expenses makes good business sense, and it can be done in a positive tone. Most portable storage companies can reduce their expenses by 5 percent by just being more cost conscious. A cost savings campaign starts with promoting the effort internally. Typically, company owners are aware of how they can operate more efficiently; however, asking for the employees' input may shed light on new areas where there are opportunities for savings. Also, keep the cost savings theme in front of your employees and yourself. Stickers, buttons, T-shirts, etc., with a suitable message may sound funky, but it goes a long way.

A routine review of cost categories on an annual basis should occur in every business. Paying attention to the smallest amounts is key in an industry where revenues are reoccurring. A minor change of revenue or expense multiplies in relation to the size of your rental fleet and the length of the average rental period. As they say, "the devil is in the details."

Balance Sheet Gymnastics: Using the Best Depreciation Methods

ANDERS NORLIN

I visit lots of NPSA members. Because our business is finance, I can compare how different companies use different accounting methods. Most companies are privately held, so the accounting is designed for owners to keep track of their businesses. This is different than accounting designs for investors or publicly owned companies. In the latter cases, the financial reports represent the manager's reporting to the shareholders.

I find that the typical company pays attention to the profit and loss statement and very few companies pay attention to their balance sheets and cash-flow statements. All three reports are equally important when presenting the company to an outsider, such as an investor or a bank.

The balance sheet is a snapshot of the assets and liabilities of your company at one specific time (typically month, quarter, and year-end). The balance sheet is the report that shows the financial strength of the company and requires special attention.

The largest asset in a portable storage company is normally the container rental fleet less accumulated depreciation. This number can vary depending on what depreciation method is used.

Each owner decides which depreciation method to use and for what purpose to use the financial reports. Most companies only use one balance sheet format. However, I suggest using three: one for the management of the day-to-day business, one for banks and investors, and one for tax purposes. This might sound like a lot of work, but it is rather simple.

Management Books: Keep the value of your container fleet at cost so that you can see what you paid for an individual unit.

Hence, keep your asset ledger for the container fleet at unit level so that you can see the cost for each unit. This is especially valuable when you are selling containers.

GAAP Books: GAAP stands for Generally Accepted Accounting Principles. They are accounting rules that are established with the purpose of giving a similar financial picture of all companies regardless of industry. Furthermore, GAAP provide guidelines to CPAs so that they can audit or review companies in a standardized fashion. GAAP accounting allows banks and investors to review financial reports produced in the same format and reviewed or audited in the same way.

However, GAAP is not always clear. For the portable storage industry one issue is the expected economic lifetime of a storage container. According to GAAP, all assets should be depreciated over a period that is representative of its expected economic lifetime. We all know that a storage container can last a long time. How long depends on where it is being used and how it is being maintained.

Portable storage operators, when talking to a bank or investor, will benefit from emphasizing the long economic lifespan of containers. You should do that in a convincing way with supporting information. It is not good enough to say that you have owned the container for five years and it still looks the same as when you bought it. A good way to present convincing information is to look at the depreciation policies of the public companies in our industry. I would say that if we used their depreciation methods as an industry standard, then NPSA members would have an easier time to obtain good bank financing.

As you can see in the chart above, Mobile Mini (MM) uses a long depreciation period. A 55 percent of original value equates to a very high residual container value. Since MM is publicly traded, the company is scrutinized by investors and is under SEC regulations; so, this is a good reference to use.

Tax Books: Let your CPA run the tax books in the CPA's systems. It is a much more complex way of accounting, especially if done on a per-unit basis. These books are not reflective of how your business is doing.

The Accounting System

Run your accounting system (QuickBooks, Peachtree, etc.) according to the management books so that you can keep track of your business day to day. When it comes time to produce GAAP books and tax books your accountant can make adjusting entries. Most likely you are only going to need these reports a few times per year. However, make sure they are done in separate systems. The easiest way is to export your management books in a table format and let the CPA take it from there.

CHAPTER 9

Strategic Planning

IT'S EASY TO JUST GO THROUGH THE MOTIONS of running your business: answer the phone, take care of customers, get invoices out, collect money. We are all guilty of this. But it can be critical mistake.

Carter Carburetors started in 1908 like most first-generation automotive companies—as a bicycle shop. The owners innovated the first brass carburetor, which metered fuel much better than anything else available. They developed a waterproof carburetor for Jeeps. They built the first ever four-barrel carburetor (1952). They built the venerable Quadrajet. But the company closed in 1984 when fuel injection replaced carburetors. Carter Carburetors ended with an empty factory.

With today's fast changing consumer landscape, we all could end up like Carter unless we get out of the daily routine. We need to see what is happening in the world and understand our customers' needs.

Economic Slowdown, Recession, and Depression: Do You Have a Strategy?

ANDERS NORLIN

The media is full of bad news. Every day, week, and month, the news indicates uncertainties in the economy. There are changes, as we all know, but are they as drastic as the media lead us to believe? I don't think so. People still have jobs. Products and services are plentiful. The ATMs are working, and the banks are open.

As a business owner, you most likely have a plan for what to do in the immediate future. But, do you have a long-term strategy? Probably not. Typically, a small business is managed on a day-to-day basis. There is no plan for how to tackle the future or deal with changes in the general economy. A strategy will help you work on the strengths you need to preserve and deal with the weaknesses that limit your prosperity. It is hard to give your own business a bird's eye view, but it can be done. Here are some suggestions.

Where are the problems? Where are the opportunities? You should look at your business and try to assess your exposure to problems as a result of changes in the economic climate. It is important to deal forcefully with the elements of your business that seem to be failing. The initial step is obviously to identify the areas that are changing in a negative way. The second step is to identify new opportunities.

Look at Customer Groups

When construction is down, you want to be conservative. Work on the assumption that containers will be returned from customers in the construction industry. Construction is never completely dead; there are always repairs and building maintenance and infrastructure that have to take place. You can assume that some rental units will go back out to the same industry, but not many.

When retail sales are down, consumers are holding back on spending. So, retailers will require fewer containers for their merchandise. However, there are exceptions. Low price leaders such as Wal-Mart and TJ Max could have increased sales because penny pinching consumers prefer to shop at the big box retailers rather than at the fancy mall. The small retailers will probably continue to rent containers, provided they stay in business. The cost of renting a container compared to renting a warehouse or building new storage space is minimal, so if your container is part of a retail operation, it is likely to stay there.

Although a general economic slowdown can affect all industry groups, the construction and retail industries often experience a more pronounced impact. What is your exposure to these two industries?

Expect other industries to slow down as well, so pay special attention to your slow-paying customers. During hard times, instruct your salespeople to visit the sites of slow paying customers. Ensure that the boxes are there and talk to the customers about their payment situations. It is important to have a feel for the customer's circumstances; visiting and talking is better than sending past due notices. If you have reasons to believe that a slow paying customer is going bankrupt, make sure your rental agreement is clear and allows you to take back the container without dealing with a bankruptcy trustee. The latter can be a long and tedious effort with no other benefit than getting your own container back while having to take a loss on the receivable.

Opportunities in Dark Times

There are times when doom and gloom are a commercial reality. But it's also a commercial reality that opportunities are out there all the time. The flipside of an economic slowdown is that many people may need more storage space for unused equipment, machinery, furniture, and other bulky items. Times will turn good again, and so portable storage is an excellent solution for riding out the economic storms.

For the same reason, customers may also look for more offsite storage (containers rented from you and stored at your facility) than they previously did. If you can offer storage at your site, economic downturns could be a better time than ever for this service. Start to promote your new services nearby. Canvas your industrial neighborhood, look for opportunities, and talk to the local leasing agents. They usually have a good feel for who is looking for new space (smaller or larger), as well as who is moving in and out of the area.

Be Ready for Change

If you start to offer offsite storage, think through your business model and make sure you differentiate between the two products. New situations may require new routines. Customers are going to want to visit their containers to add or remove items, so you have to assure their safety.

Second, you have security issues. You need to know who is visiting a customer's container. Managing that is easy if the owner shows up, but it is trickier when the visitor is an employee of your customer, or someone else who says they are authorized to enter the customer's container. Therefore, keep a log of who is going in and out and when, and what container they go to.

Customers may also store items that you don't want to have in your yard, such as chemicals, paint, explosives, and other harmful items. Make sure you give the customers guidelines as to what they can and cannot do when your facility is open. Inform your staff of your routines in dealing with this new customer group. Finally, talk to your insurance agent so that you have the proper coverage for the added business.

In addition to looking over your own business, look outside of your company. Talk to your vendors, suppliers, and customers. Keep them abreast of your situation and expectations.

Because there will be turmoil in the financial world, it is extra important to talk to your bank. Provide them with information frequently. It is better to be proactive than reactive. If your banker hasn't been to your facility, invite him or her over and demonstrate how you operate. Most companies in our industry function very well. We have internal routines and controls. We may not operate as formally as a bank or large company, but in most cases, we work with high standards. Your banker should get a good understanding for how you operate on a regular day.

Assess your local competition. Are there opportunities to buy any of your competitors? Most likely an established operator is not going to want to sell during a time of economic downturn. However, some companies could have customers that are primarily from the construction industry. If so, they could feel an economic slowdown more than you. Second, if you know that a competitor has paid premium prices for their containers, then they will struggle as more containers sit idle (off-rent). It is also difficult to sell containers if the market is weakening.

Conclusions

During tough times, take a bird's eye view of your business and develop a strategy to deal with necessary changes internally. Then look for opportunities outside of your company. The good times always roll again. We just don't know when.

Manage the Process, Not the Events

PHIL HERNDON

When we first started our rental business, we were constantly running fire drills to get equipment into our yard, painted, decaled, delivered, and billed. Our Friday afternoons were often spent running around trying to fit the pieces of our business together and make it work. We had a "just in time business" almost every day! Then, late one day, someone asked why we had to *react* to everything.

In the heat of battle, it is often difficult to see just how wasteful a reactionary operation can be. So, we began to establish processes and worked to minimize the fire drills. Here are four areas that have helped us.

Supply

Keep a supply of extra rental boxes on hand, regardless of the season. I know some rental companies that always try to keep no less than 10 percent of their fleet on hand. Small operators can't afford to have stacks of available inventory on hand for the next phone call, but that shouldn't stop us from being ready to set a rental box on a delivery truck when the phone does ring!

Part of the supply challenge can be overcome by purchasing the right equipment. If the equipment we buy can be used as a rental, sale, or a modified box, then we have conserved cash and planned for opportunities.

Additionally, we buy ahead for paint and decals. Don't let ten 40-foot rental boxes stacked up outside your office make you hold back on ordering more paint. We make our own lock boxes, which is always a good shop-time filler. Staying ahead of demand saves time later. We can install lock boxes, paint, and add decals fast when we have all those components ready and on-site.

Communication

Good communication between staff will improve workflow. If the shop staff doesn't tell you that a stack of rental containers needs to be cleaned, which leads you assume they are ready to rent, your company will be in a bind when a school system orders thirty units. To improve communication, we have a centrally located white board that lists what is lined up for shop work. Maintaining that board keeps us on course and watching for how we can best utilize shop time while keeping the rental operation adequately stocked.

Sometimes, internally, we talk too much about what we are doing. But that is much better than having isolated staff members with conflicting agendas!

History

We value our historical rental information. It helps us stay ahead of customer demand, makes us proactive in securing business year after year, and challenges us to fill in the slow times. For many of us, the larger portion of our customer base is seasonal. It is critical that you anticipate their business so that you can serve seasonal customers for years to come.

A repeat customer has a relationship with you. They know what to expect, you know they pay their bills, they don't abuse your equipment, and they are already set up in your database. It makes sense to pursue them every year. We just had a box come off-rent and the customer thanked our driver with a very nice bottle of wine. Good customers are nice to have and easy to keep if you manage your business in a planned fashion.

Define Your Business (and Don't Save the Planet)

Preparing starts with defining your business! We all get that frantic call from someone who urgently wants to rent what you don't normally offer. Even if you could meet the caller's needs, we are usually better off not supplying that customer. Customers who don't plan ahead are usually not ready when your delivery truck arrives, and they usually don't keep the unit for as long as they intended. They are often slow payers who forget to call for off-hire pick up. Don't try and help these people! We have learned that we are better off by not getting sucked into a customer's fire drill caused by that person's poor business practices. With that said, we try to help people however we can, provided it is not at the expense of planned regular business.

When you are away from the office, it is rewarding to hear your staff say that everything is going well. That means that the processes needed for building the rental business are happening! Work on establishing effective processes and the equipment will go out on-rent!

Managing a Business During Economic Storms

ANDERS NORLIN

It's hard to run a business when the news is always negative. It affects your spirit, your willingness to take risks, and your staff. Here are some hints to help you manage your business during challenging times.

Accept the Value of Work

People will adjust to lower expectations about what they do and how they are remunerated. More people will appreciate that they "just have a job." Furthermore, during economic downturns, people find more satisfaction in doing a good job than how much money they make. The appreciation of having a job and of doing a good work will improve employee satisfaction, which makes businesses better.

Maximize Talent

Company owners need to get the best out of their employees. Use a recession to challenge your workforce and see who can help your business grow stronger. If you are forced to lay off people, make sure you take good care of those who remain and take on more responsibility. Those who stay can't feel punished because others left. Help employees understand what is expected of them, train them for their assignments, and hold them accountable for their positions. Creating a team spirit is more important during challenging times than ever. Good people work because they feel rewarded by progress, not necessarily by a paycheck.

Be a Leader

When bad news hits, the business owner must demonstrate leadership skills. Being an owner or "the boss" isn't a guarantee that you are viewed as a strong leader. It must be earned by building trust and by making meaningful changes. You need good information to make critical decisions. Communicate frequently with your staff so that you get honest feedback about what is working and what isn't. Talk to people in other industries so that you have a better understanding of what is going on outside your sphere.

Form Alliances

Look for opportunities to enter business relationships with other companies that have a complementary product. Classic alliances in the portable storage business are with fencing and portable toilet companies. However, there are many more businesses that have products that can benefit from being delivered in, stored in, or built into a container.

There are different types of alliances. A sales alliance is when two companies agree to sell complementary products and services. A solution-specific alliance is two companies that agree to jointly develop and sell a specific marketplace solution. A geographic-specific alliance is when two companies agree to jointly market or co-brand their products and services in a specific geographic region.

Work on Personal Development

If business is slow and you have more time available than normal, look for ways to invest in yourself and for ways to improve your business. Take a computer class, freshen up your high school Spanish, or learn about new methods that can enhance your business. Don't ignore your personal life. Now may be the time to shorten the "to do" list for your home. Being active and having a sense of fulfillment makes it easier to have a positive outlook. An economic slowdown is, after all, a reflection of what people believe about the future.

Plan for a Brighter Future

Focus on the day-to-day impact of an economic recession on your business but manage for the long term. In the short term, you may need to cut costs; however, for the long term you should invest. A recession is a good time to invest because prices are low, sellers are pressed, and creditors are cleaning out.

A wave of uplifting news can change the sentiment of your customers in a positive way. So, avoid being overly conservative.

When the economic tide turns for the better, you should be ready to serve your customers. Otherwise they'll end up going to the competition. If that happens, those customers are most likely gone forever. On the other hand, be prepared for another severe downturn. We have seen "bear rallies" in which the stock market goes up while the economy continues downward. In those scenarios, times usually get tougher before they get better.

What does this all mean for a portable storage company? Well, most of it is common sense. First and foremost, take good care of your customers and your employees. They are the most valuable relationships for your business. Assume responsibility for finding ways to improve the business. As a small business owner, you are "it." You are the leader who everyone will look to for help when things don't go well. You are the entrepreneur that built the business by having the desire to succeed and grow. During times of economic decline, your management skills will be challenged to cope with the turmoil. Stay positive, keep your customers happy, and look for new opportunities. The future is always bright.

Did I Hear the "R" Word?

PHIL HERNDON

Say what you want about our second President Bush, but he had a remarkable ability to hold his course in the face of critics and contrary data. Global warming and weapons of mass destruction are just two examples.

As small business owners, we must recognize that the economic environment around us will impact our companies. However, we don't have to be victims. We can't ignore recessions, but they should not hold us back from continuing to build our businesses.

During the major crisis that started in 2007-2008, our rental business slowed considerably. We worked in our shop four days a week. On some days, it seemed as though very little revenue generation happened. As the owner sitting in the captain's chair, I sometimes wondered if I would have a company! These times of hardship can have a positive result if we use the slow pace of business to our advantage. Let's consider some ways to do that.

Don't Slow Down

In my days as an outside sales rep, I found that I could talk myself into a slowdown. A few customers would tell me about their slow businesses, and then radio news would give me a report about downward economic trends, and before I knew it I was not feeling the urgency to make my five sales calls that day. Don't let negative news become self-fulfilling! If you keep in touch with customers, watch for opportunities, stay focused, and keep your energy up, you will weather the storm and be better positioned to respond to the coming upswing.

During a recession, one of our good customers had gone silent for two months. I assumed it was due to the economy. I didn't feel like hearing another story about how bad business was. Finally, I called the customer and learned that a competitor had come in and undercut my price! Ouch, lesson learned. I adjusted our price and am now waiting for that customer's next order.

The Benefits of Less!

My teenage daughter's mantra is: "More money, more trouble." In some ways I agree. When revenue is up, we tend to lose control and ignore waste. So, economic downturns can help us focus on reducing expenses. It doesn't take a Harvard MBA to know that when revenue declines you have to cut costs. Here are some of the costs we have reduced:

Vehicles: We turned in a leased pickup truck and replaced it with a sedan that gets twice the mileage. The monthly lease payment was reduced by $100.

Telephone: We finally looked at our phone bill and found that unused features had piled up many unnecessary expenses. We knocked $200 per month out of the phone bill! Cell phones make us money because customers can reach us anytime. But I looked at our plan and made changes that saved another $40.

Service intervals: We have a sewage pump service, fuel delivery, and trash removal. We switched the pump service to twice a month. Anyone of these services can add up.

Office Equipment: We converted all our printers to black and white laser. As a result, the cost of operation is much cheaper than inkjet and we don't miss the color printing. Also, using QuickBooks Online and Google Calendar reduces software expenses while providing mobile ability and multi-user access.

Office Supplies: I never thought once about the cost of mailing envelopes. Then I found I could have envelopes delivered to us for $25 a box, a savings of 50 percent compared to the $50 we had been paying to the warehouse office supply across town!

Insurance: We changed to a medical savings plan and increased our plan's deductible. Even with the medical savings account, we have reduced our medical coverage costs by 10 percent. We did this while giving our employees and their dependents more control over how they use the benefit. We recommend that you meet with your insurance agent to discuss options for liability, workers compensation, and auto.

Credit Card Bills: Spend some time and go line by line through your monthly bill. I recently talked to an NPSA member who found a reoccurring monthly charge for a service he hadn't used for a year.

Financing: It is a double benefit when you can plan for the long term as you reap short-term gains. We did some refinancing that allowed us to pay off a note five-months early, reduce some other monthly expenses, and end up with a net monthly cash savings.

Reducing the Cost of Goods: We analyzed our expenditures on welding supplies, paint, steel, and everything else used to repair or modifying a container. I found dust masks at half the price we had been paying! We have reviewed our steel purchases to make sure that we get the best value, and we make sure that we use the minimum amount of material. We are more aggressive at scheduling our pick ups and deliveries. One strategy is to delay off-hire pickups as long as possible in hopes of a convenient on-hire to match.

During economic downturns, operators usually buy fewer containers. But this provides more time to look for the best box at the best price. A downturn is also a great time to sell or throw away unneeded things. Two mechanics and I once went through the shop to throw things away and consolidate supplies. We also found long-lost tools!

Finally, in slow times, people are looking for a deal. So, we took all the container ends we had, installed rollup doors, and sold them locally. It is real money when you don't have to buy a container to sell a container!

Dealing with Aging Accounts Receivable

To my surprise, slower business cycles have allowed us to clean up our accounts receivable. In an odd sort of way, I enjoy visiting a customer who is behind in rental payments. I tend to have good luck with bringing a check back to the office. A personal visit often works better than phone calls, collectors, or court action.

Remember to be realistic and creative. If the customer has no money, there is not much you can do. We recently set up a three-year payment program with a customer as a way to get paid without crippling them. We also found an excellent attorney who is effective at collecting and working with delinquent customers.

A Great Time to Make Changes

There may not be a better time to change phone systems, accounting software, or yard/office locations. Learning a new system or wholesale process change is easiest when you can focus and manage the change. Quieter times offer that opportunity.

Think about the things that have hassled you when you were too busy to fix them. Slow seasons can be a great time to place your older rental boxes into a separate stack, relocate the shop air compressor so you don't have so many hoses laying around, or standardize your billing so it is less time consuming.

Give If You Can

When you have to cut back, it's hard on your employees and on you. Thankfully, our shop guys are okay with working four days a week when necessary. They understand that they are fortunate to be working.

We know several less fortunate guys who went through a time of unemployment. So, we paid one of them to upgrade the sound system in our 20-foot delivery truck. He got some needed grocery money and we have nice sound in our truck. We also once hired a friend to do some marketing for us. It started out as a way to help him, but we saved a lot by using him. Helping those in need is a good thing.

Plan for the Recovery!

Economic hardship doesn't last forever. You will have to gear up before you know it. Be confident that you have used a slow economic period to your benefit rather than wallow in the negative news and data.

Be sure to keep your cash or credit facilities available. Soon enough, you will be buying boxes and putting them on-rent. You don't want to be caught with empty pockets. As the economy ramps up again, you'll be leaner and meaner!

Customer Service in Challenging Economic Climates

ANDERS NORLIN

The portable storage industry is about thirty-years old. In its infancy, people rented containers directly from the depots in their original colors. Today containers are painted in neutral colors. They have the operator's logo and phone number positioned in highly visible, strategic places. The containers have been improved with lock boxes, raised handlebars, varnished floors, extra vents, etc., to accommodate portable storage customers.

These improvements are the result of increased competition. Competition has made portable storage operators pay attention to how customers are greeted. Competition has improved the cleanliness of delivery trucks, and it has encouraged drivers to wear uniforms and engage in friendly ways with customers. So, we have gone from just supplying containers to providing portable storage containers with great customer service.

In challenging economic climates, it is important to maintain excellent customer service. Service is the tool with which a portable storage operator can most easily compete. Customers that need portable storage want an easy process. They want to talk to a knowledgeable salesperson who understands the issues involved with delivering, placing, and picking up a container. Customers want a simple credit application process, payment options, and prompt delivery. Containers are, after all, a commodity. Customers will only rent containers when they need extra storage. So, to get more business by changing the price is a waste of revenue potential.

Therefore, when you look at how to trim costs and adjust to a tougher economic environment, don't cut down on service. You can make a strong argument for why more resources should be allocated to service, even when revenues are declining. If companies are dealing with plummeting sales and sinking employee morale, the skittish customers will want more attention, better quality, and greater value for their money.

Those same customers are also aware that, in hard economic times, their patronage is vital to you. Customers with money to spend in recessions will expect to be treated like kings. If you have good salespeople who have been delivering well during normal times, don't let them go if sales are down during a weak economy. Instead, reduce your back-office staff and have the salespeople handle more tasks. They are the interface between your company and your customers. If you let them go, they will not be there to pick up new business when the economy turns positive again. Even more important, you absolutely don't want your good salespeople to work for the competition, so make sure you keep them around.

Flex Your Workforce

You may wonder how you can improve customer service when the economy is down, especially if office staff has been reduced and the salespeople are multi-tasking. One of the simplest ways to do that is to increase the hours your business is open. With today's technology, it is easy to have phone calls routed to several places. You can arrange a schedule among your staff so that customers who call early, late, or on the weekends are forwarded to someone from your company who can take a call. The same can be done with Internet monitoring. When you have an internet inquiry, don't send an automated message; instead, send a personalized message and follow up with a call. By arranging an on-call schedule with your employees, your staff can attend to business opportunities that come during non-traditional office hours. To make the service even better, extend your delivery hours to evenings and weekends. You may have to cross-train some employees to make this happen, but you'll find that to be an additional benefit for your business.

Take Care of Your Staff

Layoffs and uncertainties in a company are some of the most demoralizing experiences employees can have. Therefore, make sure that you take good care of those who remain with you after you have had cutbacks. Pay extra attention to the people on the front line: those with customer interaction. Customers, vendors, competitors, and others who interface with your company will get their impressions from the frontline people. If their spirits are good, the company image stays good. Cater to your employees in tough times. They are there to help your business become better. If you can't do that with money, make sure you do it by taking interest in them and their personal situations. It isn't only your company that is having a tough time when the economy is down; the employees and their families feel it, too.

Invest in Simple Technology

A recessionary period may not be the time for you to invest in a state-of-the-art communication system but making basic improvements that help you improve frontline service is important. Customers probably don't pay much attention to the recorded message on your automated phone system but playing nice music when they are on hold is better than silence. Spend a few dollars on a personalized message and you'll find that it results in more positive customers.

Prioritize Your Customers

In tough times, it will be difficult to give all customers preferential treatment. Therefore, pay attention to repeat customers and those who can shift more of their purchases to you. You don't have to shower your customers with gifts but let them know you appreciate their patronage with a personal phone call or send a greeting card when it is least expected. A personal touch goes a long way.

Finally, here is something for you to think about and try in your business. "When companies come up with simple, low-cost ways to trim expenses while improving service for their customers, they're likely to win in good times and in bad."

Ratios: Measuring Your Company's Well-Being and Progress

ANDERS NORLIN

"How is your company doing?" That is a very different question than, "How is business?" The latter question seeks a subjective assessment about your expectations and perceptions of the market, the industry, and your personal goals. The former question, however, should be understood as, "How is your company doing compared to other companies?" The best way to answer that should with ratios. In other words, by using meaningful terms that can be compared between different companies. Comparing your company with other companies in your industry provides valuable information about your business operations compared to the rest of your industry.

There are five common categories of ratios used to analyze businesses:

1. Growth
2. Cost control
3. Turnover
4. Profitability
5. Risk

These ratios provide vital information about the financial status and direction of your company. They help you make decisions for the future and they allow outsiders who don't understand your industry to understand how your company is doing in an objective manner.

How to Use Ratios

Ratios can be used to provide a snapshot of your company, but they are better used as measurement tools. For example, when people look at accounts receivable, which demonstrate how cash from the day-to-day business comes back into the company, most people focus on the dollar volume of the receivables and what is outstanding for a given period. That routine is key to the day-to-day business, but looking at the accounts receivable turnover ratio, at regular intervals (see below), tells us how good we are at collecting our receivables.

Likewise, we can look at the operating cost going up or down and based on that, have an opinion of how the company is doing. On the other hand, the Operating Expense Ratio, see below, will tell us how efficiently we run our business. Needless to say, looking at this ratio at different times will tell us if the efficiency of the company is changing or not.

Which Ratios to Use

We all look at our businesses differently. Investors, bankers, suppliers, and authorities will assess our businesses through their typical lenses. Therefore, select and use a few ratios that make sense to you and use them for a few quarters. See if they are meaningful. In other words, do they help you correlate changes in the business?

The typical owner/operator has an understanding for how the company is doing. The ratios should be a confirmation of that understanding. If the ratios are giving different indications than what you assumed, they could be waving red flags for emerging changes. Find out from outside parties that have interest in your business what they want to see and establish the relevant ratios for them as well.

In addition to the typical financial ratios, I'd like to recommend that all portable storage companies use the following ratios as tools to measure efficiency and growth:

- **Fleet Utilization Percentage =** total number of units on-hire / total number of units in the rental fleet
- **Average Rental Rate =** periodic rental revenue (twenty-eight-day or monthly) / average number of units on-hire)
- **Average Rental Term =** total number of days on-hire for the current rental fleet / number of units on-hire

These ratios are specific to our industry, but they tell you a lot about how your business is doing and can help you compare your business to other companies in the industry. Furthermore, they can be easily understood by interested parties outside of the portable storage industry.

The portable storage industry has matured so that companies can be compared to each other. Outsiders need to understand how portable storage companies are doing compared to companies in other industries. An owner can still measure the status of his company by looking at his yard. He can conclude that an empty yard equals high utilization. He can know that lots of cash in the bank means that business is good. But more sophisticated measurements are required.

Below is a list of different financial ratios that give vital information regarding a business. Identify the ratios that are consistent with your company's strategy and those that are consistent with the economic cycle. Then apply them to your business for a period. I'd say that a year, on a quarterly basis, is required to obtain meaningful information. Make a habit of including these ratios with your financial reports and compare the numbers between different time periods.

Most often the owner/operator is so caught up in day-to-day operations that he misses the vital information provided by the history of his own company. The history is your scorecard and foundation for moving forward. Combined with your experience, documented or undocumented, the history is a vital tool for moving your company into the future.

Growth Ratios

Revenue Growth Percentage is the percentage of change, up or down, in the revenue that your company generates during a period. Since companies in the portable storage industry often generate revenues from sales of containers, one should use the net sales revenue in calculating this number.

Earnings Growth Percentage is the percentage of change, up or down, in the profitability of your company during a given period. Changes in the revenue growth percentage tell us if business is up or down in revenue terms. Changes in the earnings growth percentage tell us if the profit is up or down. By comparing the revenue growth percentage to the earnings growth percentage, we can see how the change in profit relates to a change in the revenue. In other words, if the revenue grows by 10 percent and the earnings grow 10 percent, then it is a direct correlation. What we like to see is a positive correlation; in other words, the earnings growth percentage should increase more than the revenue growth percentage because not all expenses should increase as a result of the revenue increasing.

Cost Control Ratios

Gross Margin Percentage is the percentage of measurement of the difference between the cost of what we sell or produce versus the sales price we obtain for our products. In the portable storage industry, we often talk about making $100 per container sold. While the

$100 may be a good deal on a trade, the gross margin percentage can vary widely depending on whether the container cost is high or low. For example, the gross margin ratio, when selling a container at $2,500 and making $100 based on a cost of $2,400, is 4 percent. The same ratio, when selling a container at a price of $1,300 based on a cost of $1,200, is 7.7 percent. The formula you'd use for this number is:

- **Gross Margin Percentage =** (sales revenue – cost of containers) / sales revenue

Operating Expense Percentage is a ratio used to compare your operating expenses relative to sales in any given period. The ratio is a helpful tool in measuring how well you control your variable expenses. Do they correlate with the swings in the sales revenue or do you have efficiencies / inefficiencies in your operations that relate to the sales volume?

- **Operating Expense Percentage =** operating cost / sales revenue

Net Operating Profit Percentage is a ratio that tells you how much of your revenue translates into profits. In other words, if sales are $10,000, how much of that becomes profit that can be reinvested in the company after all expenses are paid?

- **Net Operating Profit Percentage =** net operating profit / sales revenue

Turnover Ratios

Inventory Turnover is a measurement of how many times in a period you sell your inventory. The ratio is a good indicator of how much money you have tied up in the inventory you use for buying and selling containers. The higher the ratio the more efficiently you use your working capital.

- **Inventory Turnover Ratio =** cost of goods sold / average inventory

Accounts Receivable Turnover is a measurement of how long it takes to collect your accounts receivable. This index is helpful in understanding how fast you can make your payables. If the ratio says that you collect your receivables in an average of sixty days, you will not be able to commit to making your payables in thirty days unless you have access to another source of cash, such as a credit line.

- **Accounts Receivable Turnover =** (average accounts receivable / sales revenue) *365

Profitability Ratios

Return on Investment Ratio is a measurement of the return on the money you use in your business.

ROI = net profit / average total liabilities and equity return on equity ratio is a measurement of the return on the equity you have in your business.

- **ROE =** net profit / average equity

Risk Ratios

Current Ratio Factor indicates your company's abilities to meet its short-term financial obligations. The higher the ratio the better. If the ratio is one, it means that you collect receivables as fast as you have to pay payables. If it is less than one, it means that you must have cash from another source to make your payables, and if it is more than one, it means that you could make your payables and have cash left over.

- **Current Ratio Factor =** current assets / current liabilities

Debt to Equity Ratio measures how much of your own money you have in the business. It tells you how much you have at risk versus what lenders have at risk, and it tells you how you can handle challenging times.

- **Debt to Equity Ratio =** total debt / total liabilities

Know Thyself!

PHIL HERNDON

Most people know who Socrates was because of one guiding principle he taught: know thyself. Our businesses are, in many regards, a reflection of who we are. Our businesses are demonstrations of how we convert thoughts, ideas, and actions into revenue.

Today we are constantly hammered with formulas for getting what we want. People present us with countless methods to accomplish goals, each with the same underlying message: fix thyself!

Sorry to wax philosophical, but to be your best is to be yourself. However, that principal is often lost in our businesses. So here I want to focus on us as operators, to help us discover how we can capitalize on who we are. I want to make some points that may cause some to have a negative reaction, but please don't take this personally.

Suppliers

Earlier this year, I was offered some equipment. When I heard the price, I quickly remarked that this was what I was selling for. The supplier shot back that I needed to raise my price.

Then, just this last month, I purchased a significant amount of equipment from a supplier only to learn that they, a major leasing company, were offering equipment retail through a thinly disguised website. I figured it out by matching the physical address. To add insult to injury, this company will not let me pay with a credit card, but they will let my retail customers pay with a card!

What is going on? Is the retail side of this business really that good? Do my wholesale suppliers assume that I make such a huge margin that they need to compete with me? To them, I say "know thyself"!

We all have made our journey to "single-siteness" along different paths. I sold containers as a dealer for many years and then had the opportunity to establish a rental fleet and physical yard. For that I am thankful and would not want to block anyone else trying to do the same thing. But when a supplier becomes a competitor, I think they are suffering from an organizational identity crisis. You can't be in my locker room at halftime and then play against me in the third quarter (go Ducks!). I have always admired Textainer and Triton for not accepting credit cards or selling to customers who do not have a resale certificate, principles they have held to for fifteen years. They know themselves!

Customers

Most of our customers know themselves. They are business people who know that service, quality, and dependability come at a cost. I have heard people suggest that we are in a commodity industry, that a 20-foot storage container is the same regardless of how it's provided. I disagree strongly. Storage sales or rentals cannot be reduced to an Amazon-type transaction, at least not for the customers I have. There are too many issues. My customers need more than just a fill-in-the-blanks transaction.

As I write, we are in the process of delivering four containers to a customer who has very specific requirements for delivery and pick-up timing, order of delivery, and type of box—and this is just a four-day rental. However, it is our third year in a row to provide this equipment. As with many of our customers, the plan is to do this again next year. This customer is smart enough to know the potential negative impact of another company offering lower prices.

So how do we handle the customer who becomes the competitor? The short answer is: differently. I'll bend over backwards for a good ongoing customer who values our product and service and pays the invoices I send. But when a customer changes roles and competes with me, I treat them like I would any competitor. When it is clearly beneficial for me, I do what I can to take their customers away and retain my book of business. It's not personal, it's professional. Hey, I know myself!

You

We all know that person who last year was deep in this venture and who this year is doing something else. Next year, something is sure to bring another new and different opportunity to this person. This type of wandering usually produces meager results. But for the single-site guys who have years of building our businesses, we know the value of sticking to the basics and not letting ourselves get diverted away from the core. Consistency pays off with strong professional relationships that last years.

Those who attended an industry roundtable at the NPSA annual conference heard from many little guys (and gals) about how we capitalize using our hands-on operating abilities. The Phone

Doctor sessions taught us to engage the customer, to develop relationships, and not to let price be the determining factor. I needed a reminder to treat each incoming phone call as a real opportunity rather than an interruption to my day. It makes a big difference. Especially for us who do it all. We need to know ourselves!

Act on It!

Look over the list that follows and think about how you can capitalize on who you are to get the business you want. Keep in mind that there are people who wish they could provide the service you do.

Big Rental Company Says:	The Single-Site Guy Says:
"We need you to sign this contract before the box is delivered."	"When you have time, fax me the signed agreement; the box should be there as scheduled this afternoon."
"Tomorrow delivery? I'll have to check dispatch and see if we can fit you in."	"I can make tomorrow work, but my truck can drop a box at the site this afternoon. Would that work for you?"
"Our system is set up for only twenty-eight-day billing."	"Normally we bill every twenty-eight days, but I can set up billing however you like. Monthly? Quarterly?"
"Our rental boxes are gray."	"For an extended rental period, we can be flexible. I can provide gray, beige, or the original box color. What did you have in mind?"
"If we move the rental box to another site we will have to create a new rental agreement. I'll write it up and send it to you."	"No problem, I'll update our records and the next invoice will have the reposition cost added in."
"Thanks for calling. Who are you with?"	"Hey, thanks for calling. Will you be doing this again, just like last year? Yep, Joe will be delivering the box again."

Remote Seller Says:	The Single-Site Guy Says:
"I have three boxes for sale in that location."	"We have three to choose from. What elements of condition are critical to you?"
"I'll check with the depot to make sure the box is windproof and watertight."	"I checked that box since it rained yesterday, and it is dry; in fact, if there is a leak in the first six months after you receive the container, I'll come there myself and fix it!"
"I'll ask the depot to take some pictures."	"You'll have pictures of the box in five minutes. What's your email address."
"I'll call the delivery company and see when they can get the box to you."	"You're close enough. We should be able to squeeze in the delivery. What day works for you?"
"He hasn't delivered the box yet? I'll call and find out what the problem is."	"Sorry I should have called. He got hung up in his first delivery and it has pushed back our schedule a bit."
"A hole? The depot said it was windproof and watertight. Can you patch it?"	"Ouch, I checked that box myself! These things happen. When is a good time for one of us to come out and repair it?"

When systems, procedures, and policies take precedence over hearing what a customer needs, it's no fun. We don't need to "check on it," ask for an approval, or see if we can fit it in—we own the company! Customers want to talk to decision-makers, so let's remember to talk like one.

I recently got a call from a distributor who needed a volume of raw material stored at a job site, but due to a variety of constraints this was more than just a simple drop of two 40-foot containers for two-month rental. After listening to the distributor's requirements,

I came up with a proposal that included source loading the product and then setting the loaded boxes at the job site. His email response to me was: "This is great. You made my day on this deal. Talk to you tomorrow." I do want to talk to him tomorrow and next week and next month, that is how we build our business, by being ourselves.

Technology: The Good and the Not-So-Good

PHIL HERNDON

"I fear the day technology will surpass our human interaction. The world will have a generation of idiots." – Albert Einstein.

At times I wonder if we are close to Einstein's prediction. These days, too many people would rather interact with an information processing device than an information generating human being! Some of us prefer people over machines. We limp into this age of technology wishing that we could get it to work for us! I don't know how to set my home alarm system, set the clock in my car, reprogram my TV remotes (four of them), or get my Fitbit to sync with my scale and computer! I feel like I am surrounded by technology that is delivering 50 percent of what was promised. So maybe I am Einstein's idiot?

Considering the scope of this book, I want to look at technology and how we use it in our businesses. The fact is, technology has created opportunities and efficiencies that were unthinkable twenty years ago. However, technology has reduced the opportunities to talk to customers, vendors, and fellow employees. As I write this, our office is quiet except for the tapping sound of three keyboards. Maybe soon we will get a robocall asking us to update our Google listing!

Customer Communication

We send about 70 percent of our invoices to customers via email, and we use email for about 50 percent of our outgoing quotes and process. Many transactions occur without ever talking to a customer. It seems like the best chance you have of talking to us is by not paying your bill. However, most of the time we leave a message on a machine!

It's a fact that technology expands our ability to handle more customers, but it's also a fact that our ability to build relationships and better serve customers is greatly restricted without person-to-person communication.

Recently, I talked to a regular customer, a small contractor. When I asked about her special-needs son, she was in shock. In a defensive way, she asked how I knew about her son. I explained that her husband had mentioned the son several years ago. She settled down. This example indicates that privacy concerns have gone a little too far and that the ability to be familiar with customers is slipping away.

We are developing a society of isolated individuals with fewer and fewer people who talk to each other. Companies like Amazon have reduced customer service to a series of electronic transactions. Until technology can find a way for us to really connect with each other (and I don't mean Facebook), it will only get worse.

Money

As my company grows, I appreciate getting paid through automation. You might read this and wonder why I would say that after I just said we are all becoming more isolated. To me, money is different. Getting paid or paying someone has long been a no-interaction transaction. Thanks to technology, our customers have five ways to pay us, of which three can be fully automated. This makes for good efficiency. Scanning checks remotely beats the heck out of watching a teller add up my deposit and give me a piece of paper to prove that I left the checks at the bank. Additionally, technology has provided effective ways to audit and track financial transactions, and that keeps us all honest!

It's clear there are emerging technologies, such as Apple Pay and others, that will continue to change things; but what we have today is much better than what we had many years ago, when every company had a safe bolted to the office floor.

Delivery and Pick Up

Technology has provided some useful tools in this area of business. Electronic dispatch, global positioning, and cell phones all help the pick up and delivery process. Furthermore, technology can't take away the customer meeting when the driver delivers the container. Our drivers know the importance of being the face of the company, and we get regular positive feedback on their skill and politeness. You can't get feedback like that without being face-to-face.

In my opinion, GPS navigation has its deficiencies. We have noticed that since our cell phones started telling us where to drive, our drivers have lost their sense of direction and can't recall deliveries by street or customer name. It used to be that we drove past the convenience store and then made a left on the second street, and the box was up the hill on the right. Today we do what the phone tells us, and the box is delivered!

Marketing

Once upon a time, in the early days of cell phones and outside sales, I had to be in front of five customers a day. Between face-to-face calls, I used the drive time to talk to anyone else I could get to answer the phone. Today we mine databases collecting email addresses and then send out blasts to unseen and unknown potential customers, most of whom get frustrated at all the spam in their inbox! I hardly consider that improved efficiency!

Proactively reaching potential customers is a lost art. It now seems that they reach us through referrals and websites. This feeds into my "isolated individuals" premise. We prefer an email over letting someone visit us to talk about what they offer. Email is obviously more efficient, but it doesn't allow for organic information exchange.

Certainly, technology has more benefits than drawbacks. Its benefits have been felt in every area of our lives and businesses. But Einstein's quote above is a good warning. As we increasingly interact with things rather than people, we lose. The biblical quote, "Iron sharpens iron, so one man sharpens another" is ancient wisdom that stands the test of time. But I'd still like to get my TV remote to work right!

The Greenback's Fluctuations and Your Company

ANDERS NORLIN

If you turn on the TV or pick up a newspaper, you can't escape the news: The greenback's value is constantly fluctuating. Faced with the strength of the Euro and the growing power of China, which is the leader of populous countries that are becoming important world financial powers, the dollar has weakened in the past. Policies within the US also cause the dollar's value to rise and fall.

The obvious question this raises is how will economic uncertainty affect the container industry? If the dollar is weak, as it was in the recent past, the supply of containers will decrease as US imports decline and exports increase. In this way, the strength of our currency is an indicator for the international trade and container imbalance. But eventually the pendulum swings in the other direction. As the dollar stabilizes and regains strength, the supply of containers will increase.

What this means for owners of portable storage companies is simple: don't panic. Remember that the portable storage industry is healthy, with revenues growing by double digits every year. Take a look at the big picture, and don't make drastic changes in your business strategy.

If the supply of containers to purchase from maritime leasing companies and shipping lines dries up, portable storage companies are forced to hold back on fleet expansion plans. The good news is this type of squeeze can lead to higher rental rates in subsequent months. That trend should improve the return on investment for the owners at the expense of not being able to service local demand.

We've been through many economic cycles. Back in 1995, for instance, the US dollar tanked against the German mark and other leading European currencies, causing great concerns as foreign investors flocked to buy US blue chip companies, such as Chrysler and Citicorp, at bargain prices. Furthermore, import and export patterns shifted, and the container surplus in the United States shrank. But within a few years, the situation stabilized and even reversed, with containers fetching exceptionally low prices amid a worldwide recession in 2001-2002.

We have also previously faced a challenge from several strong trading partners with influence over our country. The introduction of a single, strong currency for the continent of Europe has complicated our overseas financial relationships. The euro has challenged the dollar to become the currency of choice for international trade. What is there to stop the markets of international commodities from trading in euros instead of in dollars? It may not be as simple as changing a setting in the computer, but it is easier to change now than it would have been when Europe had more than fifteen different currencies.

Another factor in the current equation is what had been happening in Brazil, Russia, India, and China (BRIC). China is the leader in an emerging group of these populous countries that are projected to be part of the leading economic nations in the future. The People's Bank of China had been buying dollar nominated bonds to maintain our currency at a level that benefits Chinese exports to the United States. This enabled us to buy labor cheaper in China than anywhere else, and still obtain relatively good quality products. Therefore, the laws of economics take over, and production moves to China.

Traditionally, we can expect the production of goods to move to the market with the devalued currency, which in some cases is the United States, with foreign investments following. In theory, we might see Mercedes made in South Carolina rolling on the autobahn in Germany and the Airbus being assembled in Wichita, Kansas. At one point, we saw large foreign investment in Citicorp, and the German national airline, Lufthansa, bought almost 20 percent of Jet Blue Airways.

In about 2005, the cycle was a little different. Like 1995, the United States again became a cheap place to invest. But it was not cheap enough to lure the main exporter—China—to the United States to move production here. Instead, the Chinese Central Bank maintains our currency so that we can continue to import products from them.

It's important not to overreact to the devaluation of the dollar. The World Economic Forum produced a publication called "The Global Competitiveness Report 2007–2008," in which eleven thousand executives of leading companies worldwide were interviewed. They ranked the United States number one, as the most competitive country in the world. China wasn't among the top ten. Although 2.6 percent of those interviewed cited foreign currency issues as a challenge, a far greater percentage (15 percent) said taxation was the biggest challenge they expected to face in 2008.

Taking all these factors into consideration, I don't believe that a weak dollar poses a threat to the health of the portable storage industry. The secret is to adjust your business to each economic climate. Adjust to the fact that there will be times when there is a limited supply of containers. If you are in a strong, diversified market, try to take advantage of the slow season and buy container equipment during the months from January through March of 2008.

If your local economy feels like it is slowing down, buy containers only when you can rent them out at good rates and for longer periods. You need to be cautious because the economic slowdowns have ripple effects. Your customers may feel a slowdown from their customers, limiting their ability to pay you in a timely fashion.

Although it is unrealistic to expect that the portable storage industry will remain completely untouched by what is happening in the real estate and construction industries, and on Wall Street, the portable storage industry typically remains strong in the long term. I don't hear many complaints from the portable storage companies I talk to. With luck, the situation will stay that way if the operators stick to business basics. First, avoid losing money. Second, deal with people you trust. Third, talk to other businesses in your area. An economic outlook, good or bad, is nothing other than a large number of people who believe the same thing.

Set Up an Advisory Board!

ANDERS NORLIN

Most companies in the portable storage industry are privately owned and operated. This means that the owners and their families are the only people with full insight into the business.

Most likely there are times when you wish you had an opportunity to discuss your business with someone who could give an unbiased and objective counsel. To have meaningful conversations, this person needs to have some insight into your company, insight into the local economy, and industry knowledge.

However, it is unlikely that you'll find all those qualities in one person; therefore, you need a group of people to talk to. An experienced advisory board can help your business grow and prosper because these individuals are equipped to guide you toward reaching your goals. Your CPA, attorney, and banker, may seem like good choices, but they are vendors who don't share your objectives.

An advisory board is an informally organized group of suitable individuals who provide business owners with support, advice, and opinions. Contrary to a formal board of directors, which has legally defined responsibilities and fiduciary duties to shareholders, advisory boards have no formal power or legally binding authority. In other words, you are still in control. You listen to the Advisory Board, but you make decisions as you see fit.

Why Would I Want an Advisory Board?

The advisory board offers the following:

- An unbiased perspective on the economy, markets, and trends
- Structured, internal accountability, and discipline
- Credibility with lenders, vendors, and customers

- A sounding board for major decisions and investments
- Supplemental expertise to current management
- Networking and exposure to other business environments and industries
- Crisis and transition leadership in the event of unplanned management changes

Who Do I Select for My Advisory Board?

The advisory board supplements the skills you and the management of your company have. Therefore, start by looking for the competencies you'd like to add to your company, such as marketing, legal, logistics, finance, supply, operations, information technology, etc. Look for candidates that understand business and not necessarily the portable storage industry. A variety of industry knowledge on the advisory board is preferable to having members from one industry. If you feel that you'd like to have someone from the portable storage industry on your advisory board, pick someone from a region where you don't compete. Don't invite anyone who can't provide an unbiased view, such as family members, retained advisors, or members of your management team. If you are planning to make major changes, such as selling the business, handing it to another generation, opening up new branches, or adding partners, look for candidates who have expertise in these types of situations.

How Many Members Should I Select?

Most companies in our industry are relatively small. So, having an advisory board with two to five members, excluding the company owner, is probably a good number. The size of the advisory board should be determined by the capacities that are needed. For example, if you want legal, financial, scientific, and engineering input that requires four people, then four is a good number.

What Should I Expect from the Advisory Board?

First, you should require commitment; being an advisory board member means being involved, present at meetings, and engaged in the tasks at hand. In your selection process, it is important to make this clear to the candidates. Secondly, don't expect the advisory board to have all the answers. Many topics that arise are new to the advisory board members and the owner. In these situations, it is the aggregate experience of the advisory board members that is valuable.

Finally, expect to be candid with the advisory board members, and respect their opinions even if they are not what you want to hear. It is more valuable to have an advisory board that questions the owner and the management rather than vice versa.

How Do I Invite the Candidates?

Define the skillsets you are looking for and make a list of potential candidates. Approach them individually, preferably in person. You can start with just two or three people and hold an informal meeting during which your thoughts and objectives are formalized. Your initial candidates may know other suitable candidates who you don't know or haven't thought of. Don't rush to fill your board with members; it is an evolutionary process. You may find that some candidates don't meet your expectations. You may find that some don't have the interest they first showed, and you may meet new people who are suitable. Usually people are enthusiastic and feel honored to be invited. However, it is a time commitment; it is important to find members who have a sincere interest in serving on the board.

How Do I Get Started?

First, you should educate the board members about your company and its unique situation. Begin by bringing up issues that concern you most. For the board members to be able to talk to you about your issues, they need information. Therefore, present the data you use to gauge the status of your business. This might include an organizational chart, financial statements, utilization data, advertising agreements, customer and vendor lists, market conditions, etc. Once they understand the situation, they can give you feedback, thoughts and suggestions.

The Board Meetings

Hold your meetings three to six times per year. In the beginning, it is important to hold the meetings at your business location so that the board members can become more familiar with the company. Later, some meetings can be held via phone or off-site.

At the initial meetings, give the members time to get to know each other. Ask the board members to prepare a presentation about themselves, their backgrounds, and how they think they can contribute. Everyone should be informed of each member's background, expertise, and capacities.

Establish an agenda that is partially reoccurring and provide reports that are consistent and measurable. Make sure your board members are well informed of the upcoming agenda. It will give them a chance to prepare and contribute well. Keep in mind that you live with your business whereas the advisory board members are there only a few times per year. They need to be informed of the current situation and reminded of how it compares to the situation at the last meeting.

Ask the board members to give their views of current events as a way to get the meeting started. There is a lot of correlation between most businesses, so knowing what other companies and industries are experiencing can help you better understand the challenges your company is facing. Make sure there is a social aspect to the meetings as well. Have a coffee break or go out to lunch or dinner. Meetings often continue in an informal way during social events, and many decisions, suggestions, and ideas are better dealt with in a less formal environment.

Compensate Your Advisory Board Members Appropriately

An advisory board's efforts, over time, are expected to improve your business. Compensation for board members should address three things: the time they spend, the expenses they have, and the benefit they provide. There are many variations of a compensation structure: a fee for each meeting, ranging from $500 to $2,500; a monthly retainer ranging from $1,000 to $3,000; a combination of the two, as well as compensation based on the company's performance.

There is a debate about having a performance-compensated advisory board. Advisory boards have no fiduciary responsibilities, so they don't face a downside situation. Therefore, compensating them for upside or percentage of profits may encourage the advisory board to make recommendations that are too risky for the owners. On the other hand, not having an element of performance compensation may mean that the advisory board members are less engaged.

To establish the compensation, you may have a discussion with the advisory board members and jointly agree to the structure, or you as the owner can decide alone. In preparation, talk to your paid advisors, the CPA, the attorney, and other company owners. Most likely you'll be able to find a compensation package that is suitable for your company.

Challenges with an Advisory Board

Commitment to the task is essential, but you'll find that the commitment will vary. You may be faced with a board member who wants to run the company his way, or who uses his expertise in a way that is not beneficial to the company. By contrast, you may encounter board members who don't show enthusiasm or engagement. Another challenge occurs when advisory board members don't get along.

Despite a thorough selection process, these problems may not present themselves for some time. If this happens, you need to act swiftly. Confirm that other advisory board members, as a group or individually, see the same problems you see. If so, you have to decide about how to fix the problem. Usually, pointing out the problem to the board member in question is the best start. If the problem doesn't correct itself after a while, then you need to find a replacement.

To keep the advisory board effective, the owner should communicate regularly and share the same information with all board members. If information is withheld, for whatever reason, the advisory board members will lose trust in the company and quickly lose interest in their task.

How to Make the Advisory Board a Success for the Company

- **Take advantage of the advisory board.** As the owner, you spend time and money to set up this board. Use the members' expertise, knowledge, and experience, not only at the meetings; contact them as you see fit.
- **Respect the members' expertise and experience** even when it disagrees with your own thoughts and preferences. You engage these professionals to give you a second opinion; a viewpoint contrary to your own may avoid a costly mistake.
- **Communicate with the board.** Stay in touch after the meetings. Provide detailed material prior to the meetings and provide frequent information about your company and the industry.
- **Hold regular meetings** and set the dates far in advance so that all members have a chance to arrange their schedules. However, don't hesitate to arrange extra meetings if issues arise unexpectedly.
- **Have an objective for each meeting;** present an agenda and pertinent information in advance so that the board members have a chance to prepare themselves.
- **Be patient.** The benefits of having an advisory board are not instant. It takes time for the owner(s) to implement change and to see the rewards.
- **Assess the benefits of the advisory board on an annual basis.** Does it meet your expectations? Do you have the right mix of experts? Are the board members committed to the task?

Conclusion

Most privately held companies don't have an advisory board. Therefore, developing an advisory board will give you a competitive advantage. There is tremendous value in having objective, expert advice from committed individuals who share in the success of your business. Start thinking about an advisory board today!

A New Year, a New Decade: What Next?

ANDERS NORLIN

As I write this article in 2010, a few hours into a new decade, I am trying to figure out what the rest of the year will look like. During the last week of 2009 we were inundated with information about the year and the past decade along with projections of what the new year might bring.

The press seems to focus mostly on the financial world: what stocks or bonds to buy or sell, which industries and which international markets one should invest in, etc. Obviously, we'll never read in the *Wall Street Journal* or *Financial Times* about the portable storage industry. At least not in the context of what the future will bring. However, we can translate the financial projections from the mutual funds and investment banking industries so that it becomes one of the tools for running a portable storage company. It has always been my view that the portable storage industry follows the main flow of the economy, perhaps with a lag of a quarter or two. There are obviously exceptions.

Here are some quotes that apply well to our industry:

- "The best performers will be larger-cap companies with free cash-flow generation fortress balance sheets, significant exposure to foreign markets and in some cases good dividends" (John Goode, of Davis Skaggs Investment Management).

- "Many stable, large-cap companies with attractive dividends were not the ones investors rushed to own (in the 2009 stock rally). Many of them look attractively valued" (Ed Perks of Franklin Income Fund).
- "Today, there's no obvious catalyst. Inflation and interest rates are already low. I think large-cap stocks will hold well with the global recovery" (Gary Schlossberg of Wells Capital Management).

What I can read from the three quotes is that, as a general rule, larger companies in the US will do better than others. When real estate and banking industries are challenged, and when unemployment is high, banks are usually more restrictive with the cash and credit that is required for a business to expand. Therefore, cash-rich companies are better able to borrow money and be the leaders during an economic recovery.

Opportunities in the Private Sector

So how does this apply to the single-site guy in the portable storage industry? First, pick your targets. Knowing that large US companies usually do well, we can define the area where we ought to focus our marketing efforts. If companies like 3M, Cargill, Honeywell, Raytheon, John Deere, and Caterpillar are in your area, they are the obvious targets for your marketing, and so are their subcontractors.

The next step is to set up a marketing program so that you can reach your target customers. Hopefully you have kept the contact information from your old customers. If the upswing is going to come from the blue chip companies in your area, it is highly likely that you have already done business with them. Marketing is challenging in our industry. There is now clear seasonality for renting portable storage containers, with the exception of renting to the retailers. Therefore, design a marketing program that keeps your company name and product in the mind of the customer at the time when he or she has a need.

Do your marketing in bits and pieces. It's not feasible to send a direct mail piece every week, nor is it practical to send email too frequently; it'll just go in the junk mail box. The most efficient way of marketing has always been to display the container. Most of the time, you can only display a container when a customer rents it from you and thereby provides visibility at his location. There is no question that visiting potential customers can be worthwhile, despite the cost. Doing a little bit of each of these four methods is probably the best way. I hear of many different combinations but here are two of my favorites.

- Pay a visit to every business within a mile of your office. Containers are visible. It is very likely that every neighboring business has seen your yard. Some need to be reminded of what you do, some need to be educated. If you are lucky, some will need a container when you pay them a visit or when you follow up with an email or direct mail piece.
- Make a reason to pay a visit to your customers. Someone I know keeps a bowl of candy at a major customer's office. The bowl is replenished with a certain frequency, which creates an informal visit. Often enough, this keeps the company name in front of the decision-makers. The full candy bowl is a great way to maintain the personal relationship and be visible to the customer.

Also, don't give discounts to create demand. That is just another way to negotiate with yourself. Very rarely does anyone buy or rent a container because it is cheap. The decision to rent or purchase is driven by a need. If you contact prospective customers and offer discounts, you are just lowering your revenue potential.

Opportunities in the Public Sector

During normal economic times, federal, state, and local governments can be a large customer in all regions of the country. There are many opportunities at all levels across the country. However, dealing with governments requires extra effort. The spirit of the process is that all vendors should be treated equally through a fair bidding process. However, it doesn't work that way. There is a myriad of preferential treatments, qualification hurdles, and slow processing that sets democratic fairness aside. Despite these factors, it is still worthwhile to participate in the bidding process in markets where you can deliver. There are many websites that assemble government bids at different levels. Look at www.govcb.com, a service that alerts you about government contracts. You can try it for free and tailor it to fit your business.

Here are a few recommendations for dealing with the federal government.

- **Get ready:** First, understand the Federal Acquisition Regulations (FAR) and learn the process of placing bids. It is also a good idea to learn about what the agency wants to target. Realize that the agency will look critically at your business, your financial status, history, and track record.
- **Pick a niche:** Government agencies are required to meet various small business procurement goals. Any small business

can bid on government contracts; however, some are given preferential treatment, including: women-owned businesses; small disadvantaged businesses; veteran-owned businesses; service-disabled veteran-owned businesses.

- **Get a CCR profile:** To bid on government contracts, you need to register with the Central Contractor Registry (CCR). To register, you prepare a profile of your business explaining what it is you offer and what makes you unique.
- **Locate the contracting opportunities:** First, contact the small-business liaison within each agency. When you talk to the agency's small business specialist, understand that he or she will point you in the right direction and is not the ultimate buyer. Second, participate in business matchmaking events arranged by United States Small Business Administration, www.businessmatchmaking.com. It is an event arranged across the country where small businesses can have quick meet-and-greet gatherings with government and corporate procurement officers.
- **Sell:** The final phase is, as always, sales. You have to make a compelling argument for why you should be the selected vendor. Salesmanship is as much a part of a government sale as any other sale.

Therefore, be patient and disciplined. There is business out there, but the economy won't always cooperate. Keep marketing in focus and assign a specific time for marketing to different target markets. For example, visit neighboring businesses every Tuesday or call government agencies every Wednesday. Your discipline, efforts, and enthusiasm will pay off.

Working Productively with Certified Public Accountants

ANDERS NORLIN

Most companies have a certified public accountant (CPA) who is involved with financial reporting, tax returns, and day-to-day financial operations. However, in most cases the CPA does the taxes and that's it. I often hear people say, "We have a good CPA and we didn't have to pay much tax this year." All business owners want to minimize taxes and when the CPA tells us we don't have to pay a lot, we are happy.

Are we then unhappy with the CPA if we have to pay a lot of taxes? That shouldn't be the case. CPAs help us run our businesses in a financially efficient way, and that includes handling the taxes. I think most small business owners underutilize CPA services. This article is meant help you better understand what a CPA can do for a small business.

Tax Returns

Filing tax returns has to be done every year for the sole purpose of providing revenue for our state and federal governments. The CPA's role is to file tax returns that reflect our businesses in relation to state and federal tax codes. Taxes can't be avoided, but with proper planning and by using a CPA we can pay less tax on average.

The CPA's role is to advise you on how to make timely payments of income, payroll, and sales taxes, as well as other government fees. Finally, the CPA can provide a very valuable service in bridging the business owner's corporate tax situation with his personal tax situation. Most businesses in our industry are 100 percent owned by the operator. As a result, there is a close relationship between company's financial situation and the owner's personal financial situation.

Standardized Financial Reporting

A CPA provides standardized reports of different types. Your bank and other lenders are interested in seeing your financials so that they can assess loan risk. In this case, the CPA can provide financial reporting in a standardized format, which is the so-called Generally Accepted Accounting Principles (GAAP). GAAP helps those outside your company understand and compare the financial position of your company to that of other companies in other industries. GAAP includes the local applicable accounting framework, related accounting law, rules, and accounting standards. It is not a US government law, but rather a standardization of accounting, rules, standards, and norms for how transactions, evaluations, and depreciation should be viewed. There are three basic principles for financial reporting according to GAAP, as follows.

The financial reports shall be: A) useful to present to shareholders, potential investors and creditors, and other users in making rational investment, credit, and other financial decisions; B) helpful to present to shareholders, potential investors, creditors, and other users in assessing the amounts, timing, and uncertainty of prospective cash receipts; C) informative about economic resources, the claims to those resources, and the changes in them.

There are three levels of financial reports provided by CPAs in accordance with GAAP, which are: A) the compilation report; B) reviewed financial statements; and C) audited financial statements. Here is a brief explanation of what each report entails.

Compilation Report: The CPA becomes familiar with the accounting principles and practices common to the client's industry and acquires a general understanding of the client's transactions and how they are recorded.

After compiling the financial statements, the CPA is obliged to read them and consider whether they are appropriate in form and free from obvious material errors. The CPA then issues a standard report that says, in effect, that the financial statements were compiled, but because they were not audited or reviewed, no opinion is expressed.

A compilation is sufficient for most small private companies. However, it doesn't provide assurance that the financial statements are reliable.

Review: The CPA obtains a working knowledge of the industry in which the entity operates and acquires information on key aspects of the organization, including operating methods, products and services, and material transactions with related parties. The CPA then makes inquiries concerning such financial-statement-related matters as accounting principles and practices, recordkeeping practices, accounting policies, actions of the board of directors, and changes in business activities. Thereafter, supporting documents from banks and creditors are examined along with those of selected transactions.

A review—with its limited assurance —may be adequate for a business and/or its creditors.

Audit: The CPA gathers evidence on the reliability of the financial statements and performs "search and verification" procedures. In an audit, the CPA generally confirms balances with banks or creditors, observes inventory counting, and tests selected transactions by examining supporting documents. In addition, the CPA contacts sources outside the client organization to gather information that may be more objective than what was obtained from internal sources. The CPA then issues a report stating that the financial statements are presented fairly, in all material respects, in conformity with generally accepted accounting principles.

An audit provides a reasonable level of assurance that the financial statements are free of material errors and fraud. An audit does not, however, provide a guarantee of absolute assurance.

So, which one of these reports do you need? It all depends on whether you have reporting requirements and who you are reporting to. If your bank requires a certain level of reporting, you'll do it to comply with their requirements. If you are looking for new loans or to increase your borrowing capacity, you may want to have reviewed or audited financial statements to show the lenders that you are committed to high-level reporting.

If you have a business with employees involved in your bookkeeping and accounting, you'd want to have a review or an audit as an assurance that they do things the right way and that there is no fraud, theft, or misuse of funds. Many small businessmen say that their trusted accountant, bookkeeper, or employee embezzled money or stole merchandise. With an outsider like the CPA taking a detailed look at your books, this is less likely to happen. If you are a passive owner, you'd like to have an audit for the reasons mentioned above. If your business has investors, you'd like to have an audit for the reasons above and to limit your own liability.

The CPA As an Advisor

If you own a small business, and if you have good control of your accounting, and if you have no lender requirements, then you don't need any of the financial reports mentioned above. However, you can benefit from having the CPA as a business advisor. Most small businessmen are isolated in their own worlds (see my recent article regarding advisory boards). A CPA brings valuable knowledge that can benefit the small business owner. The CPA also has a network of local clients who can be customers, suppliers, or investors in your business.

Use the CPA to look over your routines, internal reporting, operating systems, paper trails and other essential documentation. Have him look at your overall financial situation, personal and business, so you optimize the use of capital and manage risks from a broader perspective.

Conclusion

A CPA provides three services to a small business owner: preparation of tax returns, standardized financial reporting, and advisory services. Depending on the business owner's personal preference and reporting requirements, the CPA is more or less engaged in the business. The most common services are tax return preparation and financial reporting to lenders. These services basically describe what has happened in the company in accordance to the tax codes and the generally acceptable accounting practices, none of which helps to move the business forward.

As a small business owner, you are not thinking too much about what you did in the past; your focus is on the future. Talk to your CPA about what he can do for you as an advisor. Here are a few questions you can ask:

- Is my business correctly structured? Do I have the right corporate structure that allows me flexibility, minimal tax exposure, and a good foundation for growth?
- Can my business and I benefit from new relationships with banks, insurance agents, and financial planners?

- How do I best set up a plan for future ownership of my company?
- If you engage the right CPA, I am convinced you'll see benefits that will help your business grow and help your personal financial situation.

New Lease Accounting Rules

ANDERS NORLIN

Disclaimer: At the time of publishing this book, the content of this article was accurate. Please confirm that regulations have not changed before making decisions that could impact your business.

In the portable storage business, we talk about "renting" and "leasing" containers without really paying attention to the meaning. With renting, we most often mean letting a customer use the container and pay a fee each month or twenty-eight days until it is returned. What is meant by leasing isn't always clear, but we ought to think about the difference between the two because accounting rules for leases are proposed to change.

Leasing has long been a way of providing financing for capital intensive operations at a much higher advance rate than traditional bank loans and with more favorable terms of collateralization. One main reason is that the lessor retains the asset on his balance sheet and has some tax benefits, in addition to the lease income. A lease is defined as a contractual agreement between a lessor and lessee that gives the lessee the right to use specific property, either owned by or in the possession of the lessor, for a specified period in return for a stipulated, and generally periodic, cash payment.

The current reporting requirements for leasing have allowed companies to use leverage beyond what is considered economically prudent, without informing their investors, lenders, insurers, etc. In addition, the current structure of lease payments has given disputable tax advantages to both the lessee and the lessor. Furthermore, the current reporting requirements don't show the true economic benefits of using the leased assets compared to owned assets on a company's financial statement. Finally, current leasing rules are different between countries, which make it difficult to understand the financial exposure of multinational companies.

To provide a more accurate financial picture of companies, the Financial Accounting Standards Board (FASB) and the International Accounting Standards Board (IASB) announced a joint project to comprehensively reconsider lease accounting. The two boards' stated intention is to recognize an asset and obligation for all leases as well as the benefit of using a leased asset.

Why Make Changes?

From a legal perspective, leasing is merely the "rental" of property owned by the lessor. But from an economic perspective, many leases resemble seller-financed purchases of property. This is especially true when a lease agreement contains provisions that effectively transfer the benefits and risks of owning the property from the lessor to the lessee. In a perfect world, financial statements would represent the economic substance of relevant transactions and events that affect a reporting entity regardless of the legal form of those transactions and events.

Current Leasing Standards

The accounting profession recognizes leases as either an operating lease or a capital lease (finance lease). An operating lease records no asset or liability on the financial statements. The amount paid is expensed as incurred. On the other hand, a capital lease is recorded as both an asset and a liability on the financial statements, generally at the present value of the rental payments (but never greater than the asset's fair market value). Furthermore, one of the basic criteria is that the life of the lease is equal to or greater than 75 percent of the economic life of the asset.

Lessee Accounting

Under an operating lease, the lessee records rent expense (debit) over the lease term, and a credit to either cash or rent payable. Under a capital lease, the lessee does not record rent as an expense. Instead, the rent is reclassified as interest and obligation payments, similar to a mortgage (with the interest calculated each rental period on the outstanding obligation balance). At the same time, the asset is depreciated. If the lease has an ownership transfer or bargain purchase option, the depreciable life is the asset's economic life; otherwise, the depreciable life is the lease term. Over the life of the lease, the interest and depreciation combined will be equal to the rent payments.

For both capital and operating leases, a separate footnote to the financial statements discloses the future minimum rental commitments, by year for the next five years, then all remaining years as a group.

Impact of Leasing Accounting Rules on a Portable Storage Business

First, the rules make a clear distinction between how to deal with operating versus capital leases. The operating lease is equivalent to a short-term rental, twelve months or less. They will require more complex accounting when renting containers and other equipment for more than twelve months. Second, the rules mean that all your future lease payments for trucks, trailers, cars, copy machines, computers, etc., will show as obligations on your balance sheet. That may or may not be an issue, depending on whether you have bank loans with covenants. If you do and the new lease rules make you "overleveraged," the bank could restrict use of credit lines. Most likely it will take some time for the rules to be put in place. If your banking relationship is good, I wouldn't worry about it.

Conclusion

I doubt that these rule changes will have much impact for the typical portable storage company. Companies that have financed rapid growth with leases and that don't have much equity on their balance sheets could be impacted. Typically, companies in the portable storage industry grow slowly, have low leverage, and have lease values that are low relative to the overall balance sheet. Just be clear with your customers. When you sign a rental agreement, don't call it a lease. Regardless of the length of the rental, it is still a rental agreement. Also, talk with your CPA or tax advisor before entering into any lease agreements so that there is a clear understanding of how to account for them.

Ratings of NPSA Members Makes for Better Transactions

ANDERS NORLIN

Wouldn't it be great if we could rate container vendors and container buyers? What if you could buy from a container vendor or sell to a portable storage company knowing what other people have experienced while working with these companies? Think of how you could operate your business more efficiently. Your employees wouldn't have to consult with you every time they sell a container to a member of the NPSA. Or, if you are buying, your employees would know that they can buy from an NPSA-rated vendor within guidelines that your company has set up. Even better, with a good rating, you could pay for containers on terms, rather than when they are delivered to you.

Are We Blind and Trusting?

For the most part, our industry deals with secondhand shipping containers. We usually buy them without having seen them from unseen vendors. Neither party has any idea of where the container has been or what has happened to it during the last twelve to fifteen years. Based on our comfort with the vendor, whom we have never met, and who sometimes is in another part of the world, we send money long before we receive the containers. Or, perhaps they trust us to send them money later.

Purchasing transactions in the portable storage or container trading business are based on trust and reputation. As in all industries, there are companies that have financial difficulties at times and there are companies that have bad intentions. The challenge is to buy from suppliers who have what you need, are reputable, and that value a good long-term relationship.

Outside of our industry, credit ratings institutes such as Moody's, Standard & Poor's, and Fidget's are so powerful that they can change the relative value of currencies or impact stock markets. However, these firms don't know anything about the secondhand container or portable storage industry. For the container shipping industry, the leading rating company is the Dutch company, Dynamar. They look at the portable storage industry from the perspective of maritime container leasing.

Finally, there are personal credit rating companies that rate us, individually, based on how timely we pay our loans, what kind of debt we can handle, and our personal financial situation. Experian, Equifax, and TransUnion are the rating agencies that decide if you, personally, have "good credit" or not.

Our industry needs a program that rates portable storage and container trading companies. A supplier of a service who understands our industry and our unique products and circumstances.

Container Trading Companies/Intermediaries

These companies are vendors to most portable storage companies. They purchase containers in larger quantities from the shipping lines, maritime leasing companies, or container factories. They bring them to your area of the United States or Canada. Perhaps you have met some of them through the NPSA or other events, which helps you feel comfortable sending money to them in exchange for a commitment to deliver containers to you by a deadline. If the level of trust and your financial position are strong, then there should be no need to pay in advance, except in the case of special equipment. Most often, these companies have long lasting relationships and credit with their vendors, so your payments aren't required to fully fund their purchases. This contributes to your trust in their ability and minimizes your risk.

On the other side of the spectrum is the small trader who doesn't have a long-lasting relationship or credit relationship with its vendors. Dealing with this type of trading company, if something goes wrong, means that your payment or deposit has already been spent and the trader has no leverage vis-a-vis the vendor.

Rating of Container Trading Companies

Nothing says a big trader is a good guy and a small trader is a bad guy. You could talk with fellow NPSA members about their experiences with suppliers, but what if the NPSA had a system of financial and relational accountability that members could agree to be subject to? It would serve to assure regular members of the credit worthiness and relational reputation of suppliers that were new to them.

Credit Rating of Portable Storage Companies

How do the container trading companies look at their customers, the portable storage companies? The situation is the same as above. Some portable storage companies are great to deal with and some are not. Most suppliers are in the business of leasing containers to shipping companies, and a portable storage company is a very different type of company. Therefore, a rating by NPSA of its regular members, in accordance with criteria that the vendors can understand and agree to, would give the vendors more comfort in giving terms to their NPSA customers.

It would be a big task for NPSA to assemble information from its members about vendors and buyers, information that would be needed to establish a rating system. However, it could be done, perhaps with the help of an outside credit rating company.

CHAPTER 10

Acquisition, Sale, and Transition

ACQUISITION has been like a catapult for our business. We have purchased five companies, some as small as twenty-five units on-rent and as big as 220 units. In each case the benefit to the company was instant. My coauthor, Anders, shined in this area. His industry knowledge and financial sense was preserved in what follows. We are fortunate to have this. Should you be considering a purchase, selling, or some form of ownership transition, you will find what is written here invaluable.

Acquiring a Fleet of Portable Storage Containers On-Hire

ANDERS NORLIN

Many articles have been written with regard to the preparation, evaluation, and process of selling a portable storage company. In this article, I am going to address the process of buying or selling a smaller stand-alone rental fleet. I often get questions from our readers about how to value a fleet that is being offered for sale. By fleet, I mean fifty to two hundred containers. I am addressing a fleet of containers large enough to represent a substantial amount of money for a single-site operator, but too small to represent an entire portable storage business, or that comes with the intangible assets involved in a sale. Here are some of the key factors to consider.

Type, Size, and Age of Containers

This should be easy, but it is critical to think of how the fleet to be acquired fits into the fleet the buyer already has, or how the acquired fleet matches with the typical demand in the local marketplace. For example, if you are in an urban area, it is likely that your primary product is small containers. You should think twice before buying a fleet of large containers, even if they have been out on-rent for a long time and there is no expectation of them being returned soon.

Quality and Improvements: Painting, Markings, and Lock Boxes

Make sure the soon-to-be acquired containers match your existing fleet or take into consideration the cost of bringing them to the standard of your fleet when negotiating the price. It is very difficult to have more than one standard of quality in a fleet, primarily from a customer expectation prospective. For example, if a customer sees one of your standard, good-looking containers and calls the phone number on the container for a rental, he expects the container he ordered to have the same quality and appearance.

Location of the Containers

Think of how the fleet you are about to acquire will impact the logistics of your business. One of the keys to control the profitability of transportation is to have the fleet as geographically concentrated as possible. That means shorter distances between your yard and the customer. Furthermore, it gives you the occasional opportunity to pick up from one customer and deliver to another without passing through the yard, but still charge for one pick up and one delivery. Having a few containers on rent far away from your yard means challenges with servicing existing and new customers. You know that visibility of the containers creates new business, so if the fleet you acquire is outside of your service area, you'll be faced with the challenge of accepting new customers in a new area. You then have to make some decisions: Should I service this area, or should I turn down an opportunity to rent more containers?

The Origin of the Containers

Make sure you understand how the containers have been acquired by the seller. You want to make sure that the containers are actually his to sell. If, for instance, the seller has financed the containers with a finance or container leasing company, there may be restrictions on how they can be sold. Having the standard clause of "free of any liens and encumbrances" will give you comfort, but if they aren't, and you acquire them, you may still be dragged into a costly legal dispute.

Customer Categories and Behavior

Do your homework on the customers to make sure you understand their needs, their industries, and their seasonal behavior. There is a big difference between servicing residential customers versus commercial customers, but there are also differences within each of these segments, and a difference between how the seller services his customers and how you, the buyer, service yours.

Terms of the Rental Agreements

Make sure you understand the terms of the rental agreements. Some of the pitfalls are security deposits, prepaid pickups, and rent-to-own clauses. If the rental customers have paid security deposits or prepaid pick ups the liability that comes with the fleet can be substantial and the amount should be credited to the buyer. In a rent-to-own situation, the container(s) should be excluded from the sale. The rent-to-own agreement is technically an account receivable. Also match up the accounts receivables for each unit so you understand which customers are a problem and how they are dealt with. Secondly, you need to understand if the acquired customers pay in the same fashion as your existing customers, or if the seller has operated in a way that makes their behavior different.

Rental Rates and Billing Cycles

How do the rates of the fleet you are about to acquire compare to yours, and how do they compare to the marketplace? How are the customers billed? Are they on the same terms as your customers? In other words, if you bill on a twenty-eight-day cycle, is that how the seller has billed his customers? Are the customers billed in advance or in arrears? Is billing done on an anniversary basis or are all bills sent out at one time to all customers? How are credit card billings dealt with? If you haven't done that before and the customer base you are about to acquire expects to pay with credit cards, you must learn the rules and regulations for reoccurring credit card charges.

The Seller

Find out why the seller is looking to sell. Make sure you understand what happens after the sale. Is the seller giving you a non-compete or will he continue to compete in the same area? If the containers have the seller's name and phone number on them, will that information be removed? If so, when in the process will this be done and who pays for it? If not, will you get the phone number as part of the deal?

These points may seem trivial, but if you don't have a good handle on them, what looks like a good acquisition can become a headache.

Now onto the valuation of the rental fleet. In contrast to buying a business, in this deal you are buying a number of containers. There are two simple methods that you can use to arrive at a price that makes sense for both buyer and seller.

The Replacement Value Method

What would it cost to purchase the same number of containers and bring them to the same condition as those in the rental fleet? The costs to look at are the types of containers, the volume of containers, the cost of transport from point-of-sale to your yard, and the repair and up-fit cost (painting, lock boxing, and decaling).

In addition, you need to consider the inherent rental revenue obtained from the containers in the acquired fleet. The value of the inherent rental income is the periodic rental rate times the average rental term. The reason for using half the average rental term is that theoretically some containers can be returned the first day you own the fleet, and some will stay on-hire for a very long time. This calculation works in normal situations when the customers rent for one rental period at a time. If there are minimal rental terms in the agreements, then you should make an adjustment for that. To arrive at the number using this method you must know the total rental revenue of the fleet and have the historic data of the average rental terms. The latter requires the cooperation of the seller. You better make sure you have an idea of what that number is early in the purchasing process.

Return on Investment Method

Decide what return you want on your investment. Even if the acquired customers are flexible, customers come and go; so, you should have a good idea of current and future rental revenues. With that figure at hand and knowing the return on investment goal you set for yourself, you can come up with a value. For example, if your return on investment goal is 25 percent, then the price of the fleet should be four times the rental revenue.

Seal the Deal

To close the transaction, you need to come up with a price that works for you and the seller. Using the numbers from the two different methods is a good way to start the discussions. The numbers from the two methods will rarely be equal, so there is always an element of negotiation involved. Take a look at the tables below and see how the two methods compare in a typical market environment.

Assumptions

Container type...40 Cargo Worthy
28-Day Rental Rate $95.00
Utilization 75%
Average Rental Periods 8.00

Replacement Value Method

Container Cost	$2,500.00
Transport to Market	$250.00
Paint	$500.00
Lock box	$90.00
Decal	$25.00
Equipment Replacement Value	$3,365.00
Discounted Rental Income	$380.00
Unit Replacement Value	$3,745.00

Return on Investment Value Method

Annual Rental Revenue	$1,235.00 (13 x $95)
Utilization Adjustment	-$309.00
Net Annual Revenue	$926.00
ROI Goal	25%
Multiple	4
Unit Value	$3,705.00 (4 x $926)

In a transaction like this, the buyer is taking the risks by acquiring the revenue-generating containers and the seller is trading opportunity for certainty. To have a successful negotiation, the buyer must feel that he is buying a reasonable opportunity and the seller must feel that he is getting a reasonable value for what he sells.

Recommendations

When you acquire a fleet of containers on-hire, make sure you understand the equipment, the customers, the market, and the pricing. Understand why the seller is selling. A successful negotiation is when both parties feel their objectives have been met and the deal is fair.

To Sell or Not to Sell

PHIL HERNDON

About fourteen years ago, a good local friend asked for help. He had a sizeable dry rental fleet that was growing so fast that he didn't know what to do. He was out of operating cash and not able to cover customer demand. Through a series of events, we sold that company and did very well. Now, looking back, I wonder if I should have purchased that company? How many times larger would my business be today?

About two years after that, I purchased two-and-a-half acres of raw developable land with freeway frontage. While the property was in escrow, someone offered me 30 percent more than I was paying for the property. I sold it. Today I look back and think: What if I had held on to that property, developed it into a nice container rental/sale yard, and established a solid customer base in that area?

From these two experiences, I want to focus on seller's remorse or more broadly, the reason you should not sell your rental company. How can you be sure that selling is the right thing for you? You don't want to kick back on a beach somewhere only to be wondering why you sold!

In our industry you fall into one of three groups. The first group comprises owners who build up rental fleets just to sell them. Those people are in the minority in our association. If you are one of them, then you need not read further. Your mind is made up. It's only a question of how fast you can grow to a level that will optimize your sale price.

The second group comprises owners who have no plans for selling or transitioning out of the business. These owners have abdicated their right to choose the best way to retire or move out of the business. Maybe illness or even death will dictate the fate of the company. Maybe a surprise purchase offer combined with a negative day at the office will make the decision happen. Regardless, there is no strategy and it's anybody's guess how this will play out.

The third group comprises those who have developed a plan to optimally transition out of the company. These owners, for good reasons, have set a course that includes a strategic exit plan with winners on both sides. In this group are families passing ownership to heirs, or outside investors looking to methodically acquire the business or companies with key employees lined up to take over. These companies have built a market presence, customer and vendor relationships, and a community of employees who will not leave when ownership changes.

Why Am I in the Third Group?

Do the math. There is no better place for your money than inside your company. The simple sell question is easy to answer: I can't imagine how I could do better than I am doing in any other business. My accountant, banker, insurance agent, and neighbor constantly remind me what a great business I am in. As I write, the stock market is running flat, real estate prices are high, and interest rates are low. I just don't see any better opportunity out there.

What is your company? Sure, it includes a healthy balance sheet with a sellable group of assets. That's nice and important if you are an acquisition guy from one of the big players in our industry. But our companies are so much more than that. I look out the window at the inventory, the lifts, the trucks, and the shop, and I remember how we have built this over fifteen plus years of hard work. I think of how I get up in the morning and look forward to the different tasks that need to happen when I turn the office lights on. Most importantly, I think of the crew in the shop, the drivers in the trucks, and the staff in the office. All of them have families and full lives outside work that we help support. We have built something here that needs to be preserved and valued for its dynamic, vibrant community.

So how can you cash in on what you have built without selling out? In my case, I have willing employees who are excited about taking over. It will be a long process, but that allows for a seamless transition. In other cases, there are outside people willing to take over. Either way this is a systematic process, not a single event like an asset sale. Remember that ownership does not require that you "run" the operation; you can pull out gradually. There are more than a few NPSA owners with operation managers who handle the day-to-day activities.

I admit there are times when I think it would be easier to sell the company, buy that Tesla S, find a nice place in Hawaii, and maybe even hire a golf instructor who can patiently work with me to keep my score under 100! But then my phone rings and it's that customer who has been with us for more than ten years. Sometimes he buys and sometimes he rents, but he always appreciates our service and attention. At those times, I know I would regret selling.

Are You Prepared to Sell Your Portable Storage Business?

ANDERS NORLIN

The phone rings. It is someone calling out of the blue, offering to buy the company you have worked hard to build. You wonder, should I sell?

To answer that question, you first must ask yourself other questions. You have worked hard to build your rental fleet, anticipating a future time when you would sell or transfer the business to the next generation. But is this the right time? Do you know what you want out of the sale? Do you plan to retire outright or are you looking for a partner? In either case, what is the true market value of your company? Might there be other potential buyers who would be interested in making an offer?

It may be tempting to try and answer these questions on your own, in the long run it could be far more profitable to ask for help. Consult an industry expert with a solid track record of financial transactions and the experience of buying and selling companies in the portable storage industry, someone who understands the players and can guide you through the process. An advisor who has years of experience can help you determine if this is truly the right time to sell, and if so, how to optimize the value of your rental fleet. And if not, the expert can give you counsel on how to improve your company to make it more appealing to prospective buyers.

Developing and maintaining goodwill with potential buyers will pay off financially. Avoid unrealistic illusions that could sour a deal and instead rely on outside advice to help you define your terms.

For instance, an advisor can help you assemble the necessary data to write a prospectus that describes your company in the most accurate and positive light. An advisor should also be able to identify and attract other potential buyers to make sure you get the best price based on market conditions. And an advisor will help navigate the trickiest financial aspects of the deal to make the process a smooth one from start to finish.

Determining the value of your company is one of the most important aspects of the process. Although it may be tempting to start by asking your accountant's opinion, remember that determining a valuation is not as simple as basing your price on the intrinsic value of the physical containers, the bottom line of your P&L, or the size of your balance sheet. The value of a container rental company is the cash flow from the fleet of containers on rent, the future potential revenues from customer lists, and the market presence from advertising, promotions, and signage.

To figure out what your company is worth, you will need to consider three factors: A) the quality of your containers; B) your rental revenues; and C) the relative strength of your local market.

First, to determine container quality, you will need to evaluate your fleet's physical condition. Is your fleet made up primarily of one-trippers? Or do you also have a substantial percentage of refurbished containers? Are they clean and neat? What percentage of your fleet has signage that identifies your company and makes it easy for prospective clients to contact you? Based on your answers, an advisor can help you calculate an average overall value of your fleet. Be as accurate as possible; an experienced buyer will be able to confirm, with one on-site visit, the physical condition of your fleet.

Next, look at the sizes of the containers in your fleet and at the utilization rates. What are your average rental periods and at what rates? Assess the fleet to determine what percentage of the containers are part of the rental fleet and what percentage you consider as sales inventory. An advisor will use the information to prepare the documentation that supports your calculations and correlates with the revenue on your P&L. Typically, a business sells for three-to-five times the cash flow. Be prepared to show details of your rental revenue, your equipment inventory and your customer base compiled in the formats that the buyer has requested. Transactions of this type are usually asset purchases, meaning that the seller keeps the company and the buyer gets the assets. Therefore, do not show a prospective buyer your operational financials, unless you are selling the shares of the company. It is up to a buyer to estimate the costs of operating the business. Depending on the size of the business and its model, the buyer can operate in your market differently and take advantage of economies of scale that the small operator typically can't do.

Appraising the strength of your local market is the final step in the equation. You probably have a general idea of whether you are in a growth area where population increases are boosting demand for portable storage containers, or whether you are in a stable region. A seasoned advisor will add to this perspective by offering detailed knowledge about the macro economic climate in your area. There is no rule for how much premium a prospective buyer may be willing to pay to gain a toehold in a desirable local market. An advisor can help you assess the situation by approaching other potential buyers to determine their level of interest and comparing that to an existing offer.

If you decide to respond to a buyer's offer, then the fun starts. The initial negotiations are just the first step. A letter of intent is followed by a non-refundable deposit of a substantial amount of money. The buyer is now on the hook. An experienced advisor knows how to play the mental game necessary to complete the negotiations successfully and helps you work through the due diligence.

Keep in mind that after the buyer takes over, the negotiations will continue. Without a doubt, there will be a hold back for an extensive period of time, often in the range of 10 to 15 percent. The buyer will look to maintain as much of that amount as possible, even though it is in your interest to collect as much as you can.

You visit the doctor when you need help with your health, and you consult your CPA when you need help with your taxes. It takes a long time to sell a business, and it is emotionally draining, so make sure you get help from an industry expert.

When is the Best Time to Sell Your Portable Storage Company?

These days, you hear a lot of news about how the portable storage industry is changing. Big companies are buying up smaller companies to increase their presence in key markets. And as population growth creates new opportunities in regions across the country, new players are appearing on the scene, thanks to a supply of available capital and the ever-increasing supply of containers.

Timing a sale is one of the biggest challenges any business owner will face. When should I sell? Now? Later? Never? The answer is different for everyone and will depend on factors that go beyond personal circumstances. For example, the political landscape, the economy, and the business climate for the portable storage industry.

Politically, a new presidential administration has the potential to cause changes in tax laws that affect business. And on the economic front, periods of turmoil in credit markets may cause slower growth, thereby impacting our industry. Historically, the portable storage industry has followed the overall economic trends and is likely to continue to do so.

As for local competition, is your market becoming saturated with an increasing number of newcomers? Or do you think that the rapidly growing portable self-storage companies (PODS, Go-Mini, etc.) are taking away potential customers from you? Other factors, such as a weak dollar, may make container prices escalate as exports improve, creating a situation that changes the equipment imbalances and decreases the supply of containers available for sale from shipping lines and container leasing companies.

Meanwhile, several other issues can affect the business climate. Around the country, municipalities have been known to enact more stringent restrictions on the use of containers. Not long ago, a change in Chinese export tax laws created a longer peak pre-holiday storage season than usual, with suppliers announcing that Christmas merchandise would arrive three to four weeks earlier than usual.

How does all this affect you and the timing of a possible sale of your company? An advisor with a solid track record can help you assess these factors and, just as important, to understand the micro-economic climate in your region. Remember, for example, how the Olympic Games in Salt Lake City and Atlanta created local building frenzies that benefited the portable storage industry in those metropolitan areas.

Where your business is located is one of the most important factors in determining how profitable a sale might be. The biggest companies in the industry typically try to strategically strengthen their presence in local markets so they can guarantee a supply of storage containers to the large national companies with whom they have business relationships. Are you located in an area that is interesting to any of these companies?

Take the time to reflect on these different factors that can affect the timing of a sale. Perhaps you have been approached about the possibility of selling your business. Or maybe another owner you know is negotiating with multiple buyers. Or maybe you just want to be prepared, when the time comes, to know that it is the right time. It might be tempting to look in the crystal ball on your own, but it's best to get advice from an industry expert, someone who has years of experience buying and selling companies, and who has seen the national political and economic climate develop over time.

CHAPTER 11

Industry Statistics and Mergers

Seeing the Big Picture

PHIL HERNDON

Recently I received an email from a potential customer who made the following passing statement: "The thousands of shipping containers that, due to the imbalance of trade overseas, are clogging our nation's ports . . ."

At the risk of being a bit off topic, I thought I might use this platform to dispel this all-too-common misconception. Over the last five years, CNN and other news media, on a slow news day, will report on containers as a "blight on the US." They state that multitudes of containers are "abandoned in US ports and depots," and conclude that "we are swimming in them and no one knows what to do!" This type of reporting is irresponsible! Let's start with some simple facts.

Is There a World Container Imbalance?

Yes, but it isn't a mistake or the fault of poor container inventory management. The term "trade imbalance" is a monetary measure that hinges on exchange rates and the value of goods traded between countries. Keep in mind that between the US and Japan, the average cargo value per ton is $7,000 from Japan to the US and only $500 for cargo to Japan. But the term "trade imbalance" is not a reflection of container inventory imbalance. It's about cargo value.

Roughly 40 percent of every vessel leaving the US is loaded with empty containers. There are two reasons for this. First, if the containers are left in the US they will not be available for use in ports that have heavy export demand (China). Second, from the US we export primarily heavier, unfinished products. The average weight of a US export container is eight tons higher than that of an import container. So if you filled every container on the ship with export cargo, the ship would be overloaded. It would be wonderful if we supplied higher volumes of finished goods to the world, but we don't.

The imbalance of loaded container movement is part of the sophisticated logistics departments of ocean carriers, railroads, and leasing companies. Container inventories are not some out-of-control occurrence. They are based on seasonal forecasts and demand models that keep cargo moving to achieve maximum utilization of company assets.

Container Traffic: The Big Picture

Here are a few interesting facts about containers and container movement from 2015:

- 200 million loaded containers were moved
- More than 6000 container ships in service
- World container fleet was 17 million
- 60 percent of the container trade imbalance is between Asia and Europe/North America.

There are enough containers in the world to stretch end-to-end around the earth more than three times. If placed side-by-side, they would cover over 100 square miles of land! The 60 percent container trade imbalance means that effectively every week eighteen vessels with an 8,000-TEU capacity sail from the US back to Asia filled with empty containers! There are 2.2 containers for every vessel container slot, and that ratio has been steadily declining, which represents an increasing world container fleet efficiency (despite movement imbalances). So, from a global perspective, there are a lot of containers moving larger amounts of cargo. With the exception of auto carrying ships, almost all international cargo moves in containers.

A Smaller Picture

For added perspective, the 2007 numbers for the Port of Oakland, which is similar in size to the ports of Norfolk, Houston, Charleston, Tacoma, and Seattle:

- Container through-put was 2.4 million
- 2,058 vessel arrivals
- 1,160 containers on average, on or off each vessel
- 760 acres of container terminal supporting twenty-nine shipping lines

Compared to the numbers for world traffic, this is not so staggering; but there are almost ten thousand containers per day moving through the Port of Oakland. It's hard to imagine how all that happens. The containers you see stacked up are necessary inventory to keep goods moving in and out of this county. The massive volume of trade requires empty containers to be available in locations across the US.

Working down the chain, we come to the Oakland area off-dock container storage depots. As the industry has achieved higher efficiencies, the number of facilities and total storage capacity has fallen. Today, maybe there is a capacity of 25,000-TEUs at off-dock facilities (sorry no real data source for this). That volume represents three days of port activity, or the capacity of just three vessels. In terms of moving volume, these facilities are insignificant. But the economical repair service they provide, along with providing yards for equipment storage, is critical to the broader industry of international trade. Nevertheless, they are regular targets for those who consider containers a blight on our communities.

From this data we can draw two obvious conclusions. First, it takes a huge number of containers to keep trade moving. Second, these containers regularly have to wait in storage locations before they are used for their intended purpose; they are not abandoned or dumped. That information would be a great response to someone who suggests that your storage fleet is creating a community or environmental problem.

We also hear that containers should be cheaper and more readily available "because they are stacked up everywhere!" We repeatedly explain to people that it is not that simple. To bring that into perspective, we tell them that even with 2.4 million containers per year moving through Oakland, we once had to truck more than eighty 20-foot used sale containers from Long Beach (four hundred miles away) because there were no 20-foot containers for sale in Oakland.

We cannot expect to stop the continual misinformation and misunderstandings surrounding this critical element of our livelihood, but we can be ready with a balanced and factual response. The data here comes from a variety of sources that I can provide on request.

The Mobile Storage and Mobile Mini Merger

ANDERS NORLIN

Not so long ago, two competing giants loomed over the rest of the portable storage industry. But when Mobile Storage Group (MSG) and Mobile Mini (MINI) announced a merger, the landscape changed for everybody else. Gone are the days when both of these companies would come to town loaded with cash to outbid each other to buy local businesses. In the future, potential buyers will value a portable storage company in a more mainstream way, giving greater importance to a company's cash flow.

What will these changes mean for the smaller operator? In the wake of the merger, there will be one less competitor to worry about and one less go-to-guy to turn to if you want to sell your business. However, I think there are plenty of opportunities left for the ambitious, creative, and hardworking entrepreneurs in our organization.

So how did this merger come about in the first place? MSG had eighty-six branches in February 2008, but its fleet of 117,500 containers (an average of about 1,365 units per location) apparently wasn't big enough to compete head-to-head with Mobile Mini. Although MSG had been for sale for nearly two years by the time the merger was announced, I can't imagine that MSG envisioned joining forces with its major competitor back in 2006 when the company's leaders were promoting their business to investors. Nor do I think that the new Mobile Mini leaders had it in mind. But it happened anyway, because MSG and its owner had the flexibility and determination to find a solution. One plus one became three because two major competitors joined forces.

How large is the new constellation? I'd venture to say that the new Mobile Mini still has less than 25 percent of the market share in the United States. Since we don't have any reliable statistics, the number could be as low as 15 percent. But the point is that there is still plenty of room for the rest of the approximately two thousand portable storage companies in the country.

In markets where both companies had a presence, it is likely that either a Mobile Mini or MSG location will close to avoid redundancy. That will leave small local operators with one less competitor. That competitor, however, will be bigger than before.

We have seen years of consolidation in the maritime container side, and it seems to be good for the small operator. It opens up opportunities for niche players with specialized products and higher service levels. I think it will be the same in the portable storage container business. After Mobile Mini reduces overhead through consolidation, it will likely turn its attention toward expansion opportunities in the third-tier markets that aren't yet tapped. Expect Mobile Mini to show interest in making competition-free acquisitions in cities with good growth potential all over the country.

What else does the merger mean for the average NPSA member? First, we'll lose one member. Both Mobile Mini and MSG have been contributors to our organization in more than one respect, and that will most likely change. Second, both companies have been major buyers of portable storage companies nationwide for many years. You can probably still sell to the new company, but without the two of them competing against each other, the sale price may be lower.

In the past, Mobile Mini and MSG were both so-called strategic buyers capable of paying a higher premium than a traditional investor for a smaller company that would give them a toehold in a new market. When an investor would calculate price based on projected return, Mobile Mini and MSG would rationalize an acquisition as a way to jumpstart a new market.

Now, however, pricing of companies will be more traditional. Buyers will look more to the EBIDTA (earnings before interest, depreciation, taxes, and amortization), or in simple terms the cash flow a business generates, instead of trying to predict how much revenue a container will generate over time. With this change, our business is becoming more in tune with capital sources (Wall Street) and streamlining evaluation methods. This doesn't mean that the secondhand value of the container is ignored, but that value will have less of an impact on the price of a going concern.

There are still other strategic buyers in our markets, but no one is close to the size that Mobile Mini and MSG represented as individual companies, and none, except for Williams Scotsman, have national coverage. In addition, the race for extended national coverage, which I think existed between the two companies, is gone. None of the other large companies have claimed to have national coverage as part of their strategy.

So, what is the pricing of companies going to be? As a general rule, to price container rental fleets, the price per unit has been in the range of $2,500 to $5,000. If we tried to establish a similar rule for cash flow pricing, here is how it would work. First, we need to define what the cash flow (EBIDTA) is by calculating your annual profit, add back depreciation and interest and any income tax you have paid. Now you have a number that represents the cash generated by the business, and you apply a multiple to it. The typical multiple for small businesses is around five. Most people understand interest rate. By translating the EBTIDA multiple into an interest rate, you can see what level of return a buyer will get.

You hear numbers like three, five, eight, or twelve times EBITDA; however, these numbers can be translated into percentage rates. For example, a price of five times EBIDTA is the equivalent of a 20 percent return on investment, three times EBITDA is equivalent to 33 percent, and eight times is equivalent to 12.5 percent. I hear of sellers looking for a multiple of their EBIDTA, but they don't really understand what it means. So, by translating the EBITDA into an interest rate you can provide yet another view of the value of the business.

A seller, just like a buyer, must be reasonable in his demands. If the return on investment for a buyer is unattractive, there will be no sale. So how do you prepare yourself for the sale of your business in this environment? Well, it's back to cash flow, which means increasing the revenue and reducing the expenses. It is quite logical that higher rental revenues bring a higher price, so try to increase your rental rates and make the containers stay out longer by offering incentives. In general, more marketing will bring more opportunities, so look at what your sales staff can do better. If your rental income is $25,000 per month and you can raise it by 5 percent, you'll make $15,000 more per year and add $60,000 to $80,000 of value to your business, if we use and EBITDA multiple of four to six. On the expense side, look at what you're paying for and do it systematically by setting goals. Everyone can save 5 percent by just thinking about it, and that translates into a higher value of your business. If the annual overhead is $100,000 and you can save $5,000, the value of your business should increase by $20,000 to $30,000 using the same EBIDTA multiple as above.

This little exercise just added a value of $100,000, or $400 per container, to a fleet of 250 containers. Obviously, it is theoretical, but if you keep better cash flow in mind at all times, you'll see the results.

Godzilla Marries King Kong!

PHIL HERNDON

Tempe, AZ – February 22, 2008: Mobile Mini, Inc. (Nasdaq GS: MINI), the leading provider of portable storage solutions, and Mobile Storage Group, Inc. of Glendale, California, a provider of portable storage in the United States and the United Kingdom, today announced that they have entered into a definitive merger agreement. Under the terms of the agreement, Mobile Storage Group will merge into Mobile Mini in a transaction valued at approximately $701.5 million.

When the big guys make a huge change like this, we little operators can't help but ask, "How will this impact us?" What follows was written just after the merger of Mobile Mini and Mobile Storage Group. It shares what concerned us at the time, and what we can learn today. (Please understand that I have no axe to grind with either Mobile Mini or Mobile Storage. As with any association, there is a paradox here: These companies are fellow NPSA members, but they are also competitors.)

The merger has had numerous impacts. I've identified some of them below.

Customers

We have found that when two companies combine there are some customers who are not happy. Maybe they don't like the surviving company. Perhaps they were looking for a reason to change. Maybe their favorite sales rep was released in the merger or maybe nobody returned phone calls because employees are more worried about the merger than doing business. It's common in business to find that during transitions customers also change. This might be a good time to do some focused local marketing while announcing that you are not changing and that you will continue to serve customers.

Equipment Sales

Historically, Mobile Mini has encouraged container rental over sales while Mobile Storage (at least in my area) regularly sold equipment. With Mobile Mini as the surviving entity, it would seem likely that there will be some increase in sales opportunities for the remaining competitors in the market.

Operating Equipment

We might see some delivery trailers and yard equipment become surplus as locations are closed and overhead is reduced. Although most of us don't expect to experience a lot of rental growth this year, Mobile Mini and Mobile Storage have usually maintained quality delivery trailers and yard lifts, so there might be an opportunity to replace your aging equipment with good used equipment.

Rental Inventory

More storage equipment may become available to buy within two scenarios. Many people wonder if Mobile Mini will choose to sell surplus equipment that was older or of a less desirable type. As the consolidation of inventories begins to happen, many believe that Mobile Mini will not need to purchase equipment. One of the core objectives of this merger is to improve overall fleet utilization. Therefore, branches could be under pressure to rent out what they have rather than purchase additional inventory. So, this could translate into less demand on equipment available through dealers, leasing companies, and shipping lines.

Rental Rates

As a result of this merger, we may see rental rates strengthen. This could well be the case with national accounts that negotiate rates for multiple locations, leaving smaller operators out of the competition. It might be worth it to check back over some of the large retailers at the local level just to see if this change has impacted them. Local offices will often use local suppliers if they are aware of you and confident you can provide the service.

People

There will be some good people coming out. In the past, these types of mergers have produced a fresh crop of industry experienced people. These people come from a highly structured environment. Turning them loose in your operation may not produce results unless you are willing to provide regular direction and focus.

Locations

As they merge, some areas with duplicate locations will be consolidated into one. This could be an excellent opportunity to improve your yard location especially since you are not changing the use of the property. Moving yard locations is not cheap and it's a big hassle, so make sure it's in the right location for you. Has anyone ever had a successful telephone switchover in these types of moves?

Storage Business Acquisitions

Thinking of selling your business? From one perspective, you might want to wait. With this merger, two companies that were steady buyers are now one company. That might cause them cool down on acquisitions in the short-term. But the buying machine should come back to life. Another option is to look to other national storage rental companies. We could find them with increased growth objectives in light of this big merger. I know of two companies that are stepping up their acquisition programs.

Opportunities

Two big companies that offered "institutionalized service" are only going to be more institutional and less flexible. As small operators, we can offer customer-tailored service that the big guys cannot. For example, we have some customers who want one invoice for a specific period, including delivery, pick up, and return all lumped together. We can do that. If the customer wants one invoice per container or all containers on one invoice, we can do that.

I recently talked to a customer who had used Mobile Mini in the past but was totally frustrated because when he called to order a container after keying through the prompts in the phone system, all he got was voice mail. He really wanted a 10-foot wide unit from Mobile Mini, but after talking for a bit we rented him a regular 20-foot storage unit. In one call, it was all set up with no hassle.

Bottom Line

We little guys need to continue to do what we do best: adapt, choose our opportunities, sharp shoot our markets, and be available.

Several years ago, when two large depot operators merged (Container Care and Global Intermodal), many of us were set back on our heels. Many were saying this would be a nightmare causing service to go down and storage costs to go up. In the end, our industry adjusted to the reduced options. Most of us have forgotten the merger ever took place!

Portable Storage Meets Portable Buildings

ANDERS NORLIN

More and more, the portable storage industry is encroaching on territory that portable building companies had staked out for themselves in years past. The move makes sense for portable storage companies. By converting their containers into offices and other spaces where people can work, they arrive first on the job site of any major project and can increase their exposure.

Those advantages outweigh the main drawback of earning a lower return on investment for converted units. But don't count portable building companies out of the fight. They already have their own strategy to expand their businesses into areas traditionally dominated by portable storage companies. They see an office unit as an "easy sale" to an existing customer, an opportunity to add an auxiliary product by providing a container for temporary storage. The large modular building companies are even developing menus of products for their customers, providing a one-stop shopping opportunity for everything that is used in and around a portable building.

What effect will these maneuvers have on the members of NPSA? It's not a big deal to convert a container into an office to add value. The payoff is higher rent and more business opportunities created by offering a broader range of products. Therefore, this seems like a good opportunity for the portable storage operator to expand. But if the portable storage companies increase their product lines and compete aggressively with the portable building operators, don't expect the portable building industry to look the other way.

Caution: regulatory roadblocks ahead. One way the portable building industry can level the field is if the government starts to more rigorously enforce regulatory requirements. For now, the typical portable storage company owner who fails to comply with the rules gets away with it because his product is used temporarily and very rarely catches the attention of the state or local authorities.

Meanwhile, the portable building industry is well-regulated, with licensing requirements and established rules in place nationwide. The portable building companies seem to comply diligently with the various state and city regulations. Their industry organization, the Modular Building Institute, provides detailed regulatory information for its members in each state. By emphasizing regulatory requirements publicly, and by bringing them out in the open more frequently, the portable building industry could raise the awareness of both customers and the authorities, creating a higher barrier to entry into their turf. Complying with existing regulations could be too costly for the portable storage operator, thereby keeping him out of the portable building industry.

The portable building industry's argument goes like this: The portable storage companies have no similar retaliatory tactics to use in their efforts to keep the portable building companies from entering their turf. Meanwhile, the portable storage companies have their own challenges with regulatory issues (or lack thereof) across the country. Therefore, one could assume that the portable building companies are better suited to deal with regulatory situations for storage containers. Who knows? This issue has been dealt with more or less successfully on local levels across the country for the last five to ten years, and it is likely that the situation will remain unclear for still some time.

History 101: How We Got Here

If one looks at the two industries, it appears that their backgrounds and cultures could make them apt to deal with regulations. The portable storage industry is more fragmented, consisting of many small local operators and a few large companies controlling around 25 percent of the market.

By contrast, the portable building industry is less fragmented, with a few large companies controlling more than 50 percent of the market. The portable building industry also seems more mature and more structured. That can be explained by looking at the history of the two industries.

First, the origin of both products is entirely different. In simple terms, one could describe the portable building as a demand-driven product. The rapid population growth of the 1950s and 1960s created a need for temporary buildings to house school children, workers, soldiers, and other individuals. During these decades, entrepreneurs started to build buildings that were easy to move around. Existing building regulations could easily be applied to the new, portable structures. Obviously, new regulations were adjusted to comply with the conditions of these new movable products.

The portable storage container took another route to its market. Shipping lines and container leasing companies had to solve the problem of having an asset—cargo containers—that were not used to their full potential because of the equipment imbalance issue, as well as the lower standards required in the portable storage industry. Hence, they asked themselves, "We have this strong, stable and mobile product. What do we do with it? Who needs safe, secure, and mobile storage?" And so, the portable storage industry came about as way of dealing with a residual product.

The portable storage industry started to evolve when there were large quantities of containers coming off-hire in North America in the late 1980s and early 1990s. Existing regulations for shipping containers were not applicable to this new portable storage industry.

Apart from local city ordinances that deal with the nuisances and lack of property tax revenue, there are no norms or standards. One can see why industries with such different origins have different strengths. The portable building industry is driven by demand and has a comparable product, the permanent structure.

The portable storage container just starts to show up in many places around the country and evolves into an industry. Most likely you have been faced with the situation and know that a creative person can think of an endless number of storage applications for a retired cargo container. Needless to say, it is not difficult to understand why there are no rules or regulations for portable storage containers.

The Money Equation

From a financing perspective, an unclear regulatory situation requires additional scrutiny when seeking to finance containers converted into office space and combination office/storage units. A good financier should look at the worst-case scenario with any opportunity. "What happens if my customer doesn't pay and I get the container back?" With a standard 20-foot or 40-foot storage container, there is usually a way to find buyers. The difficulties increase with the size of the fleet that is returned, the location(s) of the units, and the utilization level.

Needless to say, the container condition and general market conditions have a significant impact as well. However, with an office unit that is not certified for its purpose in a market that requires certification, the challenges are tremendous and the options to dispose of the items limited. Who wants to buy an office container if they can't technically use it for its intended purpose? The options for the financier are to either move the unit to an area where the requirements are different or convert it back to a storage container at an added cost to an already distressed asset.

The Solution: Specialize

So, what is the conclusion of these observations? Looking into the future, I think we'll see portable building companies increasing their entry into the portable storage markets faster than the portable storage companies will enter the portable building markets. Regulations will become more of an issue. This change will have some impact for most NPSA members, except for those who very aggressively try to expand in the direction of a specialized fleet and those who stay away from including converted units in their rental fleet.

We'll see more specialized products that will be used for unique applications, ranging from mobile skateboard ramps to mobile multistory buildings. One can take for granted that the more complex the product, the larger the need for compliance with regulations and ordinances.

In addition, the more complex products will require sophisticated financing at higher rates, but with greater returns for the operator. It is most likely to the benefit of the NPSA member to educate himself sooner rather than later on the local rules, regulations, and consequences thereof for his entire fleet, and especially for more sophisticated products.

Finally, turn the challenges of regulations and financing into a business opportunity. They are, after all, hurdles that require effort to overcome. Those who don't will be left behind and those who do will have stronger and more profitable businesses.

Containers: An Art Form?

PHIL HERNDON

A few years back, a graduate student in architecture asked for some help in creating an exhibit showing her designs in alternative housing concepts. After three visits, countless photographs, and a half hour digging though my scrap metal pile, she completed her project. Later she sent me a photo of the exhibit. As it turned out there was a 2-foot, square section of corrugated container wall, with a bunch of renderings around it. She said everybody loved it!

As I sat down to dinner at a restaurant recently, I realized the wall between the kitchen and dining area was an older red K-Line container. Last week I drove past a stack of containers that was set up for a zip line. After a building burned down in Berkeley, the owner worked with the city to rebuild a restaurant constructed from containers and tents.

I would suggest that over the last fifteen years we have witnessed the elevation of our humble utilitarian shipping containers to a

nouveau chic status. They are cool. So, what has driven this surprise acceptance of this lowly assemblage of steel? I would say three things.

1. **Bigger Is Not Better:** After years of bigger is better—houses, cars, stores, and public buildings, we have reached our peak. Value is not just about size; it includes other qualities. It is pleasing to step into a well-designed space that has originality and warmth. It is fun to feel that you are in a space that is unique. Needing volumes of private space has become more of an excess than a personal goal. Remembering that first year of college sharing a dorm room that was half the size of your bedroom at home may have helped in challenging this notion of how much space I really need!
2. **Building Codes:** We have observed a shift in local building departments over the last six years. For years, the municipal planners had an automatic response to the word container: "No!" This was a simple, end-of-discussion no. Thanks to hard working architects and structural engineers, building officials and their staffs have begun to see the benefits of using containers as design elements and viable forms of temporary structures. Additionally, containers have gained acceptance as temporary structures. Considering the combination of durability, strength, and portability, the container is an easy choice for a temporary structure.
3. **The Industrial Look:** The container has a uniform design. Of the millions built each year, they all fit required dimensions. Except for color, are all them same. It's fun to take a uniform, industrial thing and making it unique. From a design standpoint the vibe starts with reuse. Although it is not totally

accurate, there is a belief that the world has too many containers. Utilizing them for building purposes is a healthy thing to do for the environment. The next part is that containers have an industrial look that exudes a feeling of security and safety.

4. **Cost:** Containers are deceptive; at the outset they seem very economical and an amazing value. However, once a contractor begins the process of converting the box into its intended new purpose the costs begin to mount. Nonstandard forms of foundation, structural support, electrical, plumbing, and HVAC, all begin to erode the value proposition of using containers. The driver for using containers in a building project should never be cost savings if there are any significant interior improvements or code compliance issues. Recently after reviewing four books written about tiny houses or building homes with containers, I was surprised to find none of them surfaced this important truth.

So, is this a fad or will it stick? And I would guess it will stick. Concepts like reuse and living in smaller spaces seem to be long-term strategies, not design nuances that will fall to a newer better concept. Time will tell.

CHAPTER 12

The NPSA

A Brief History of the Association

PHIL HERNDON

In 2001, a group of shipping container dealers gathered to discuss the challenges facing those who sell shipping and storage containers. In attendance was Richard (Dick) Honan, the owner of American Trailer & Storage, in Kansas City. Honan began to ask the question, why don't we have an organization for the portable storage industry? As he began to explore this idea, facts surfaced that clearly pointed to a need for and strong interest in an association.

There are now 3,500 companies nationally in this business, but at that time there was no industry identity. From Wall Street to Walmart, there was no real understanding of what this business provided for our nation and economy. Additionally, business operators had no sense of best practices for their companies. Each operator seemed to adapt his or her service to whatever opportunity presented itself.

In the summer of 2002, the NPSA was formed. Honan has the distinction of being the founder and first member of the association. With strong conviction, Honan began to canvas the portable storage operators seeking support and members. He hired Joel Rathbone to provide full-time focus on member recruitment, production of a newsletter, and meeting planning.

Later that year at the Intermodal/IANA Expo in Southern California, an informational meeting was held. Then, in early 2003, the board of directors began to take shape and a date was set for the first annual convention, October 16 and 17, 2003.

Defining the Industry

The business of storage comes in many forms, from massive warehouses to small safe deposit boxes at banks; storage services is a real business. Portable storage is unique in that the object that does the business of storing resides at the customer's location, hence the word portable! The work of storing is done with shipping containers, the same containers that provide intermodal transport all over the world. They are portable, durable, secure, and relatively inexpensive. Portable storage customers vary widely. The only requirement is that they have a place for the storage container.

Why Have an Association?

Before the formation of NPSA, many were asking why there should be a national association of portable storage companies. Those of us who built the organization have had to answer that question many times. Here are my top four reasons.

1. **Legitimacy.** As a business owner, I am constantly faced with competition that undercuts existing pricing, provides poor service, and leaves customers with much less than promised. It is hard to convince your customer that they get what they pay for! The NPSA is a vehicle for establishing professional relationships with solid, reliable companies that have a commitment to service and quality.

2. **Networking.** Each of us provides service outside of our normal area. Your regular local customer needs to rent equipment in another state and you need a reliable company to sublease from or refer them to. The NPSA can provide us with a network of companies we can trust. Or maybe you have a customer who is on the verge of bankruptcy. What should you do to protect your assets? You can call a fellow association member and talk through the situation, or you can call an associate member who provides financial or legal services for advice. Knowing that a potential equipment supplier is a long-standing associate member gives you confidence in their ability and service. The benefit of networking for small and medium business today is great. Don't go it alone. Learn from others!
3. **Unified Effort.** The portable storage industry has grown dramatically over the last twenty-five years. Many of us have worked hard to establish businesses that serve the communities where we live. Meanwhile, at an alarming pace across the country, municipalities have begun to reject portable structures as acceptable forms of on-site storage. Each of us has heard a customer say that the city rejected their request to locate a storage container or trailer on their own property. If we as an industry are going to successfully stem this tide, we must work together to establish a workable definition of "portable storage" in the national building codes and then work at the local level for understanding and acceptance.
4. **Future.** Business is changing! Our profession is getting more and more complicated. The old days of tracking rental inventory with three-by-five cards arranged in a rack on a wall are

> gone. In the future, business will be about *more:* more regulations, more tracking, more types of equipment, more customer requirements, and more ways to do business. The NPSA, with a strong focus on being a resource to its members, can give us the information and ability to stay up with changes so that we can confidently focus on the future.

Who Are the Members?

The NPSA has two basic groups of members: regular and associate. Regular members are those who are actively selling or renting portable storage to customers who put their stuff in storage. Associate members are those companies that provide services to the regular members.

The regular members fall into one of three groups. First there are the single-site operators. These companies have a central focus of providing portable storage in a defined geographic area. This is by far the largest group of NPSA members. The second group comprises multi-site operators, those companies that have multiple locations and cover a wide geographic area. Several of these companies are publicly traded and have more than thirty locations. The third group is made up of members who focus on selling containers over renting them. Some operate their own sales yards whereas others will sell or even trade inventory as opportunities present themselves.

The associate members fall into two groups. First, there are companies that sell storage equipment to members. These include container leasing companies, one-way shippers, and dealers. Leasing companies typically have their own sales representatives who offer equipment to the regular members. However, in some cases they will sell their equipment to dealers who in turn offer the inventory to members. The one-way sellers will purchase equipment in Asia, use it for a cargo shipment to North America and then offer it up for sale at its arrival point. Finally, the dealers purchase from or sell containers for shipping lines, leasing companies, or container factories. No single container supplier has a significant advantage over another. The market is constantly changing, which impacts pricing, equipment type, and availability.

The second group of associate members offer products other than storage equipment. These include delivery trailers, coatings, modification parts, inventory control systems, locks, insurance, or Internet marketing services.

Growing

The first annual conference was a huge success with more than two hundred attendees representing 120 companies. A full day of seminar topics led to lively discussions during and after the event. The conference social events gave attendees the opportunity to build new relationships with suppliers and fellow operators. Membership grew to over seventy-five companies. By the first month of 2004, the association passed one hundred members.

In early 2004, the board hired John Finnessy to be the executive director after an extensive national search. With Finnessy and Rathbone (serving as operations manager), the association began to reach out to current members and aggressively recruit new members.

In May of 2004, the association held an educational conference in Dallas. The two-day event attracted over one hundred attendees and was the first regional event for the NPSA focusing on operating challenges.

The second annual NPSA conference, held in September of that year, had two-and-a-half days of presentations and discussion. More than thirty exhibitors displayed their goods in the 100,000-square-foot convention hall at Caesar's Palace in Las Vegas. The first of its kind, the trade show provided the opportunity to show and see rental equipment, delivery trailers, inventory control systems, and other necessary products for the portable storage industry. By the close of this event association membership had passed two hundred.

Near the end of 2004, the association board of directors agreed to take over the Resale EXPO event from its owner, Phil Herndon, who was also an NPSA board member. The Resale EXPO had been held every other year starting in May 2001. Its focus was container dealers and their suppliers. In May of 2005, the third Resale EXPO was held in Monterey, California, attracting over two hundred attendees representing twenty countries. The three-day event dealt with container supply, maintenance, and industry economics.

In August of 2005, the association joined with one of its members, K&K International, for a reception in Baltimore held the evening before the annual Baltimore Crab Feast. The crab feast is a longstanding charity event organized by the Propeller Club of Baltimore. It attracts thousands of people associated with the transportation industry. At this event, a national consulting company presented data on the portable storage industry. The study, contracted by the NPSA board of directors, was initiated to set a baseline of data on our members and to help the association leadership understand and focus on member needs.

Shortly after this event, in September of 2005, the association held its third annual conference in Las Vegas. It was bigger and better than the previous conference. One large exhibitor remarked,

"We do more than five trade shows each year, and none is more productive than the NPSA event!" The success showed as well with NPSA membership exceeding three hundred members by the end of the conference.

In April of 2006, a second regional education conference was held, this time in Chicago. Attendance exceeded 150. The topics included information on developmental equipment tracking technology, worldwide equipment pricing, and regulatory considerations for local operators.

Once again in August, the association co-organized the "Pre-Crab Feed Reception" in Baltimore with K&K International. Then in September of 2006, the fourth annual conference was held in Las Vegas, with the keynote speaker, Rodney Slater, the secretary of transportation under President Clinton. New attendance records were set, and this event was once again a huge success.

In May of 2007, the fourth annual Resale EXPO took place in Monterey, with more than three hundred attendees. The group heard from industry leaders such as John Maccarone, chairman and CEO of Textainer Group Holdings, Ltd., and Ian Karan, chairman of Capital Lease. This event continues to gain worldwide recognition as a forum and meeting event of container resellers.

The NPSA Today

In 2001, there was no standard industry storage product or service. Anything that could pass for portable storage was used. You would see old truck bodies with tar tape covering holes being used for storage behind a store. Simple enhancements like lock boxes and paint were not the norm. At that time, I was a wholesaler and I confess that I sold a lot that was poor quality and should have never become part of a rental fleet. We have come a long way since then.

Our standard of quality has been shown publicly as a benefit to our customers. From its beginning, the NPSA has served as the vehicle for our industry to become professional with standards for equipment and services.

The NPSA's purpose is "to promote and represent the common business interests of and improve business conditions among members of the mobile and portable storage industry." Historically, the NPSA has advanced its purpose through a variety of methods, such as annual and regional conferences, a newsletter, operator site visits, a phone book, and the association website. These tools each support our purpose, but the NPSA also provides opportunities to learn from each other. Together we increase our legitimacy as an industry.

Why You Should Join the NPSA

ANDERS NORLIN

A membership with NPSA offers numerous benefits that will keep you on top of important changes, issues, trends, and legislation within the portable storage industry. There are many benefits to being a member of an industry organization. They include:

- **Networking:** In the great race to the top, who you know matters as much as what you know. Meeting industry people outside of your own local sphere of contacts has great value.
- **Events:** NPSA holds events on a regular basis. These events engage and educate the members.
- **Professional Development:** Continued education and professional development is important for all business owners. NPSA provides opportunities for you to learn from fellow members through the seminars and presentations at the events.

- **Learning Best Practices:** All industries have best practices of some kind. They may not be formalized, but by connecting with fellow members and receiving industry information from NPSA, you'll have the opportunity to operate your business in a better way.
- **Industry News and Information:** Being a member of NPSA gives you the fast pass to any noteworthy information and development in the portable storage industry. In addition, the portable storage industry is uniquely linked to the maritime container leasing industry and the shipping industry. What happens in those industries has a major impact on the supply of containers throughout North America. NPSA's events offer the members a unique opportunity to meet people in those industries from all over the world.
- **Support NPSA's Mission:** NPSA gives the portable storage industry a public voice for its members and acts as a guardian for the well-being of the industry as a whole.

You should evaluate your expectations and your benefits from the association. NPSA is primarily run by volunteers who work for the benefit of the industry, because they like it. They also see benefits for their companies and they think it is good for the industry.

Your level of engagement will have an impact on the benefits you get from your membership. Paying your annual dues and going to the events aren't enough to reap the benefits of your membership in the association. You must also participate in association activities and become involved. Being part of a committee is a path to learning more about the organization and the industry. Engagement also develops deeper relationships. That will help your business and help you grow as an individual. Furthermore, as you contribute to the organization, you help make the organization better. Finally, being involved gives you an opportunity to have an influence in improving the broader industry. (This is not a place to drive personal agendas.)

Unfortunately, like many other organizations, NPSA has an active board but not very many active committees; therefore, the board is not as effective as it could be. It would be ideal to select board members from those members who have committee background, experience within other associations, or suitable skills that would allow them to hit the ground running when becoming board members.

Some members develop informal, voluntary subgroups for various reasons. Such reasons can be related to a unique situation, a unique product line, a unique geographic area, or simply because the people involved get along well and trust each other. These groups develop naturally as people meet at NPSA events and get to know each other.

A membership in NPSA not only benefits you, the company owner, and your employees; it also projects a positive image of your company to your customers and vendors. Membership in industry associations shows initiative, community engagement, and a commitment to staying abreast of market developments.

Simply put, what you get out of your association membership is directly related to what you put in to it.

Did You Know?

- There are about eight thousand professional organizations and associations in the US.
- Approximately 85 percent of all business failures occur in companies that are not members of their industry association.

- Two of the biggest advantages of association membership are networking and camaraderie with other members.
- To reap the benefits of an association membership, you must be engaged and make an investment of time and effort in the association's activities.

What If There Was No NPSA?

First, we would never have emerged into the industry we are today. The evolution of the portable storage industry could have occurred on the shoulders of the big companies, but we smaller operators would have found ourselves lagging way behind and losing business that should have been ours.

Second, the anti-container folks would have gained strength in portraying portable storage as a blight on communities. Today the quality of our equipment and service has played a big part of holding the anti-container people at bay. Our market cannot be served with the product we offered fifteen-years ago.

Third, we have established relationships. When our phone rings and the customer is not in our service area, we refer them to an NPSA member in their area. Conversely, our phone regularly rings at the direction of an NPSA member in another area. Beyond referrals, there are the personal relationships that have developed. At the annual conference, it's a wonderful time to catch up how family members are doing and hear about that vacation someone took.

Finally, we do events very well in places worth visiting. We have had events in Napa, Monterey, Kansas City, Santa Barbara, Chicago, Lás Vegas, Virginia Beach, Orlando, San Diego, Baltimore, Philadelphia, Montreal, Nashville, Dallas, Sitges (Spain), New Orleans, and Winston Salem. All great places to visit and especially to meet good friends! Who needs to plan a vacation when the NPSA has events in such cool locations?

The Future

The NPSA continues to grow and change with the times and the industry it serves. NPSA members have recorded excellent company growth. Some have sold their companies to other member companies. Many new companies have started and used the NPSA as a resource for learning the business.

Today the NPSA holds a firm position as the only service association to the portable storage industry, and with member-leadership it will continue to serve its members and industry.